THE
ORDNANCE SURVEY
PUZZLE TOUR
OF BRITAIN

Can **YOU** crack over 300 fiendish puzzles?
Follow the clues around Great Britain to find out!

By Ordnance Survey
and Dr Gareth Moore

Mapping images © Crown Copyright and database rights 2019
Text and other images © Ordnance Survey Limited 2019
Puzzles © The Orion Publishing Group Ltd 2019
Puzzles by Dr Gareth Moore

The right of the Ordnance Survey Limited to be identified as
the authors of this work has been asserted in accordance with the
Copyright, Designs and Patents Act 1988.

This edition first published in Great Britain in 2019 by
Trapeze
an imprint of the Orion Publishing Group Ltd
Carmelite House
50 Victoria Embankment
London EC4Y 0DZ

An Hachette UK Company

5 7 9 10 8 6

A CIP catalogue record for this book is available
from the British Library.

ISBN: 978 1 4091 8471 3

Printed in Italy

The names OS and Ordnance Survey and the OS logos are protected by UK
trade mark registrations and/or are trade marks of Ordnance Survey Limited,
Britain's mapping agency.

Every effort has been made to fulfil requirements with regard to
reproducing copyright material. The author and publisher will be
glad to rectify any omissions at the earliest opportunity.

www.orionbooks.co.uk

MIX
Paper from
responsible sources
FSC® C023419

CONTENTS

FOREWORD BY SEAN CONWAY

It was April 2008 and I was curled up in my tent on the side of a mountain somewhere in Scotland. The wind was so strong that at any moment I thought I might fly Mary Poppins-style all the way back to Land's End, where my journey began. With clothes still damp from cycling all day in the rain, I lay there trying to fall asleep, staring up at the condensation forming above me. I was cold, wet, miserable, hungry and tired and absolutely loving every second of it. And so began my love affair with the best island on the planet: Great Britain.

The simplicity of putting on your walking boots, grabbing a rain jacket and flask of tea for no other reason than to follow a small dotted green line on a map to a place in the countryside you have never been to before, is one of life's purest pleasures. No smart phone, TV programme or fancy sports car will come close to what it feels like to be out in the elements, conquering your own challenges, however big or small they may be. It's become somewhat addictive for me and in the past decade I have travelled the iconic Land's End to John O'Groats route six times by five different modes of transport, including swimming, running, sailing and cycling. I have also driven it once but that doesn't really count. My OS maps have always been along for the journey and I've become obsessed with building my map library in my office and spending hours discovering new routes and trails whenever I travel somewhere new. Having the skills to read maps and navigate the outdoors is something that I feel we all need to learn and pass on to future generations. They are skills that will help us make the most of this beautiful island we live on.

As an OS Champion, I am proud to be part of a wonderful group of people who in various ways have made the outdoors a huge part of their lives. It means so much when we see others forging their own adventures and witness the confidence that brings. So grab your map, find a spot you've never been to and go and have your own adventure. Just don't forget the flask of tea.

INTRODUCTION

Great Britain is beautiful and unique, and our island is not short on variety. Our fair isle successfully crams a lot into its relatively compact geography; from the beaches of Cornwall through to the rugged beauty and tranquillity of the Scottish islands, there are so many adventures to be had and sights just waiting to be discovered.

What's your favourite part of Great Britain? For some, this may be as easy (or as difficult) as thinking of your favourite film, or piece of music. But could you justify your choices in three words? This is the challenge we set the team here . . . and it was hard. Possibly harder than some of the questions in this book!

At Ordnance Survey everything we do is designed to help more people get outside more often. This is so ingrained into our DNA that we started a social initiative called GetOutside to motivate people to discover the best Britain has to offer. We hope that this book inspires you to join the 5 million people who have engaged with us. Especially as it is well proven that an active outdoor lifestyle helps you live longer, stay younger and enjoy life more.

You can find out more ideas, tips and inspiration at www.GetOutside.uk. With over 250,000 pages of content, the site is bursting with ideas. From family activities, things to do and places to go, through to descriptions of the wild and wacky sights that make Great Britain unique, it will show you there's always something to explore either close to home or further afield.

As you journey through this book, you will also meet some of our awe-inspiring OS GetOutside Champions who will showcase their favourite parts of Britain with stories and tips. You can find out more by following them on social media or looking at the Champions' pages on the website.

But with so much to explore, where do you start? OS GetOutside Champion and endurance athlete Sean Conway might inspire you to think big, but there's no rule to say you should start training for an Iron Man or the first ascent of a mountain. You don't even need to stray too far from your doorstep. Sometimes all you need is an idea, a map and enough time to get you started.

We hope you enjoy the book and its challenges, but more than that we hope it's got you excited to find out what's nearby and beyond. So, take on the challenge of these puzzles and then take a step over your threshold . . . it is here that the greatest of prizes awaits you.

Happy adventuring!

Nick Giles, Managing Director – Ordnance Survey Leisure

AN INTRODUCTION TO THE MAPS AND PUZZLES

In building this collection of maps, it very quickly became apparent that you cannot even begin to represent the diversity of landscape, our human impact, or the rich history of Britain in just 40 maps. It is even more difficult when you try to do the same for the eight sections we have organised the maps into. Mark Wolstenholme has selected them in the same way that he would frame a photograph; by looking for a visually interesting area that was balanced on the page, with plenty of detail for puzzle opportunities and, hopefully, an interesting story to show what maps can reveal to us.

Then there are the questions which will test how far your skills will take you. There is something for everyone: a mix of word puzzles, search-and-find clues and general knowledge questions, as well as navigation conundrums to satisfy the more skilled map-readers. And with island outlines to identify, the eagle-eyed geographer will be kept entertained. The questions are split into four levels of difficulty:

- **Easy**
- **Medium**
- **Tricky**
- **Challenging**

Once you have completed all 40 sets of puzzles, you'd be forgiven for thinking you've conquered the book, but there is still one challenge to overcome: pit your wits against the master puzzle on p.186.

Hopefully these maps, puzzles and stories will encourage you to look at a map of your local area for places that have a story to tell and footpaths to explore. What are you waiting for? Put your knowledge and skills to the test all whilst celebrating the regional diversity, history and landscapes that make Great Britain so great.

COMMON MAP ABBREVIATIONS AND SYMBOLS

SELECTED TOURIST AND LEISURE SYMBOLS

The style, size and colour of these symbols vary across map series, or may be described by text with no symbol.

🏛	Art gallery (notable / important)	�اعM	Museum
	Boat hire		National Trust
	Boat trips		Nature reserve
	Building of historic interest	☆	Other tourist feature
	Cadw (Welsh Heritage)	P	Parking
Ⱦ	Camp site	P&R	Park and ride, all year
	Camping and caravan site	P&R	Park and ride, seasonal
	Caravan site	((	Phone; public, emergency
	Castle or fort	✕	Picnic site
✝	Cathedral or abbey		Preserved railway
	Country park		Public house(s)
	Craft centre		Public toilets
	Cycle hire		Recreation, leisure or sports centre
	Cycle trail		Slipway
	English Heritage		Theme or pleasure park
	Fishing		Viewpoint
	Garden or arboretum	V	Visitor centre
	Golf course or links		Walks or trails
HC	Heritage centre		Water activities (board)
	Historic Scotland		Water activities (paddle)
U	Horse riding		Water activities (powered)
i	Information centre		Water activities (sailing)
i	Information centre, seasonal		Watersports centre (multi-activity)
	Mountain bike trail		World Heritage site / area

ABBREVIATIONS

Acad	Academy	Ind Est	Industrial Estate	Rd	Road
BP	Boundary Post	La	Lane	Rems	Remains
BS	Boundary Stone	LC	Level Crossing	Resr	Reservoir
CG	Cattle Grid	Liby	Library	Rly	Railway
CH	Clubhouse	Mkt	Market	Sch	School
Cotts	Cottages	Meml	Memorial	St	Saint / Street
Dis	Disused	MP	Milepost	Twr	Tower
Dismtd	Dismantled	MS	Milestone	TH	Town Hall
Fm	Farm	Mon	Monument	Uni	University
F Sta	Fire Station	PH	Public House	NTL	Normal Tidal Limit
FB	Footbridge	P, PO	Post Office	Wks	Works
Ho	House	Pol Sta	Police station	ₒW; Spr	Well; Spring

PUBLIC RIGHTS OF WAY

OS Landranger	OS Explorer		
-----------------	-------------	Footpath	**The representation on the maps of any other road, track or path is no evidence of the existence of a right of way.**
— — — — — — —	— — — — —	Bridleway	
-+-+-+-+-+-+	+-+-+-+-+-	Byway open to all traffic	
-·—·—·—·—·—	+-+-+-+-+-	Restricted byway (not for use by mechanically propelled vehicles)	

The symbols show the defined route so far as the scale of mapping will allow. Rights of way are liable to change and may not be clearly defined on the ground. Please check with the relevant local authority for the latest information. Rights of way are not shown on maps of Scotland, where rights of responsible access apply.

PUBLIC ACCESS

OS Landranger	OS Explorer	
◆ ◆ ◆	◆ ◆ ◆	National Trail, Scotland's Great Trails, European Long Distance Route and selected recreational routes
● ● ●	n/a	On-road cycle route
○ ○ ○	● ● ●	Traffic-free cycle route
n/a		National cycle network route number – traffic free; on road
[4] [8]	n/a	Cycle route number – National; Regional
· · · · ·	n/a	Other route with public access (not normally shown in urban areas)
Danger Area	DANGER AREA	Firing and test ranges in the area. Danger! Observe warning notices Visit: **gov.uk/guidance/public-access-to-military-areas**

ACCESS LAND

Access land (symbols indicate owner or agency – see below)

 Forestry England
Forestry and Land Scotland

National Trust; always open, limited access – observe local signs

Woodland Trust Land

Natural Resources Wales

National Trust for Scotland; always open, limited access – observe local signs

Access land portrayed on Explorer maps is intended as a guide to land normally available for access on foot, for example access land created under the Countryside and Rights of Way Act 2000, and land managed by National Trust, Forestry Commission, Woodland Trust and Natural Resources Wales. Some restrictions will apply; some land shown as access land may not have open access rights; always refer to local signage.

LAND FEATURES

⁝⁝⁝⁝ ⁝⁝⁝⁝	Cutting, embankment	⋏ Beacon ⏽ Mast	
▬	Bus or coach station	� Lighthouse	
⌀	Glasshouse or structure	⏾ Lighthouse; disused	
△	Triangulation pillar	⏂ Wind pump	
+	Place of worship	⅄ Wind turbine	
Current or former place of worship;		⤬ Windmill (with or without sails)	
♦	with tower		
♦	with spire, minaret or dome	▨ Solar Farm	

BOUNDARIES

	OS Landranger	OS Explorer
National	─+─ ─ ─+─ ─	–·– ––– –·–
County	─·─·─■·─·	─·─ · ─·─ ·
Unitary Authority or London Borough	─·─·─■·─·	
District	─+─ ─+─ ─+─ ─+	─── ─── ───
Civil Parish (CP) or Community (C; Wales) n/a		· · · · · · · · · · ·

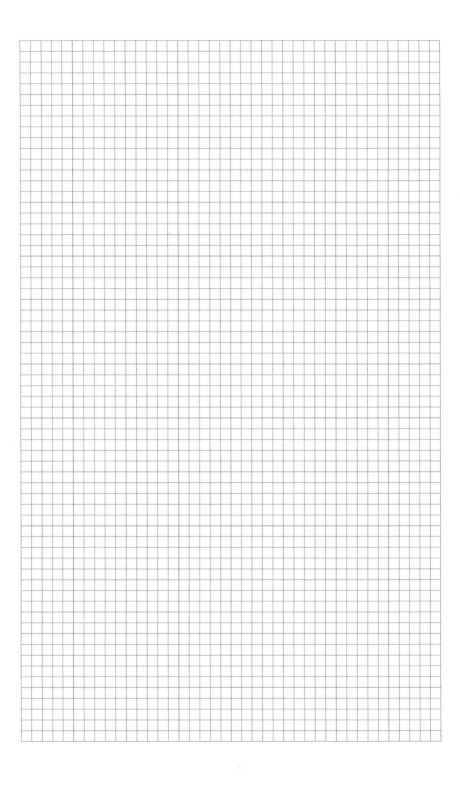

SOUTH WEST ENGLAND

1: St Mary's, Isles of Scilly

2: Swanage, Dorset

3: Athelney, Somerset

4: Widecombe in the Moor, Devon

5: Cotswold Hills

GET OUTSIDE!

Name: Lucy & Fi (Two Blondes Walking)

Who are you?

Hi, we are Lucy and Fi from the popular outdoor blog 'Two Blondes Walking'. We specialise in expedition work with young people as well as running navigation and wild camping workshops on Dartmoor. The South West boasts two unique coastlines, the distinctive National Parks of Dartmoor and Exmoor, its very own coast path and the stunning Isles of Scilly.

In three words, sum up what makes your area the best part of GB
Moor to Sea.

Your favourite walk

Our favourite walk takes us along Dartmoor's Devonport Leat to the mysterious Crazy Well Pool. Legends and wild swimmers abound at Crazy Well but you will need a map to find it. Beware of visiting on Midsummer's Eve; local lore has it that anyone whose face is reflected in the pool that evening can be sure of imminent death.

Your favourite view

One of our favourite views is from the top of Exmoor's Dunkery Beacon. We have often waited here for Duke of Edinburgh's Award teams and the panoramic views across the moor, out to Lundy Island and over to Wales, are definitely to be recommended.

The perfect day out in your area

A perfect South West day out would include a moorland walk, a cream tea in a village café and then some delicious local seafood before a night-time stroll around a harbour. There aren't many places where doing all that in one day is possible!

Why people should visit

If you haven't visited the South West yet, you are missing out. We have a mild climate, plenty of sunshine and the warmest sea temperatures in the UK!

SAND, SEA AND SHIPWRECKS

The map: OS 25-inch 1906

The story: One of the greatest maritime disasters in British history

You can't get more south west in Britain than the Isles of Scilly, a remote archipelago of around 200 rocks, islets and islands, about 45 km (28 miles) from Land's End. The maritime climate of Britain has probably influenced and shaped our history, culture and society more than anything else, if not our obsession with the weather. The Isles of Scilly are directly affected by the North Atlantic Current, giving them a very mild climate, important for their flower-growing industry and tourism. But they can also be lashed by fierce Atlantic storms and in October 1707 one such storm wrecked four ships of the Royal Navy's fleet returning from Gibraltar with great loss of life, including the Commander-in-Chief Sir Cloudesley Shovell. His grave is marked here on St Mary's, although Queen Anne later had him exhumed and interred in Westminster Abbey. The disaster spurred the authorities to set up the Longitude Act in 1714 with rewards worth millions of pounds today. From this came John Harrison's marine chronometer – now in the Royal Observatory Greenwich.

Easy

1. Can you find three rocks named after animals?

2. How many orange numbers, indicating contour heights, can you find on the map?

Medium

3. Which landmark on the map is found at the end of a magic beanstalk, according to a classic fairy tale?

4. After washing your linen, which location matches what you might hope to have?

Tricky

5. Start at Great Britain, and head around the coast to a profound position. Travel due west until you reach what is now the A3110. Now travel uphill along the road. What settlement do you come to first?

6. Begin at the second highest bench mark (BM) height on the map, and travel south-southwest to what might be AA or even AAA. Follow a line of equal height from that location until you reach the edge of a field. Turn left, and follow the footpath around the edge of the field until you reach the extremity of a water feature. What is the name of that feature?

Challenging

7. Where might you expect to find Jenna and Barbara Bush?

8. Can you find locations on the map that are anagrams of the following words or phrases? Ignore the spaces and punctuation, which may differ from those in the place names.
   a. UNCORKS
   b. ARID HOSTELRY
   c. CHIVALROUSLY SOLVES DEGREES
   d. OH, GRIM SHORE

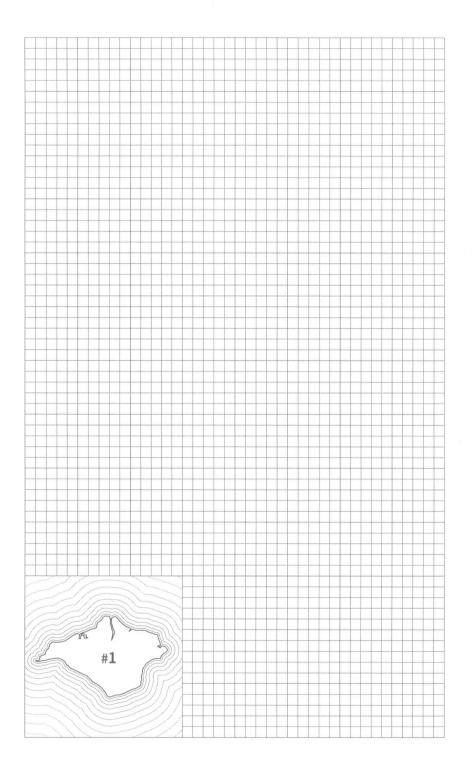

#1

MAP
2

LONDON-BY-THE-SEA

The map: Open Map Local Vector at 1:8 000 scale

The story: The stone that built a capital

Today Swanage is a popular holiday destination and a gateway town to the Jurassic Coast World Heritage Site, but its past is much more industrial particularly with the quarrying of limestone around the coast. The Romans prized the hardest Purbeck stone as it could be worked and polished like their Mediterranean marbles. The Medieval builders loved it for its strength and durability building Corfe Castle to defend the entrance to the Isle of Purbeck and leaving us magnificent buildings to experience including Salisbury Cathedral and Westminster Abbey. In the mid-19th century, Swanage mason George Burt helped his uncle John Mowlem's local construction business expand into numerous rebuilding projects in London. The limestone was shipped around the coast as the railway line to Swanage didn't open until 1885. Waste material from demolished old buildings was used as ballast for the return trip and recycled. As a result you can find lots of old London enjoying the seaside, including the front of the Town Hall (London's 17th-century Mercers' Guild Hall) and the harbour clock tower which once stood at the end of Westminster Bridge.

QUESTIONS

▨ Easy

1. How many different types of tourist and leisure symbol, marked in blue, can you count on the map?

2. How many streets end in 'Lane' (which is abbreviated to 'La' on this map)?

▨ Medium

3. In what field might you expect witches to gather?

4. Which street has a name that translates to 'good agreement'?

▨ Tricky

5. How many routes can you find from Swanage Hospital to Harrow House International College that only involve changing the name of the road you're on a total of four times? (Don't count roads you cross directly over towards your total.)

6. What word do the following four routes spell out?
   a. Head south from the southernmost church without a tower to the end of the road by the school, then turn around and turn right, following the road to the hospital
   b. Head west from the easternmost church along the A road, turning left after 175 metres. Take the first left, and at the end of the road turn around and drive back along the road. Then turn left and again left, stopping when the road changes name
   c. Start on the road to the east of the church nearest the Town Hall, then follow the road south and around the corner until you reach the first turn-off
   d. Enter the map area from the south, travelling to the end of a road named after a well-known Isaac. Take the first three right-hand turns and keep going until the end of the road

▨ Challenging

7. Which words on the map are being cryptically described here?
   a. Geometric figure is old-fashioned and boring
   b. Sullivan's partner tangles girl with bet

8. Can you find two roads with identical names, except that one has an extra letter inserted relative to the other – but none of its other letters rearranged? Ignore the road ending ('Street', 'Road', etc.) for the purposes of this question.

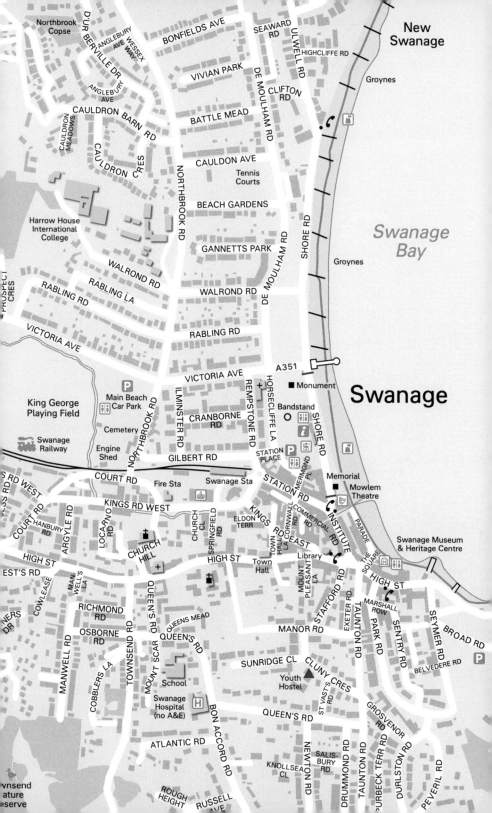

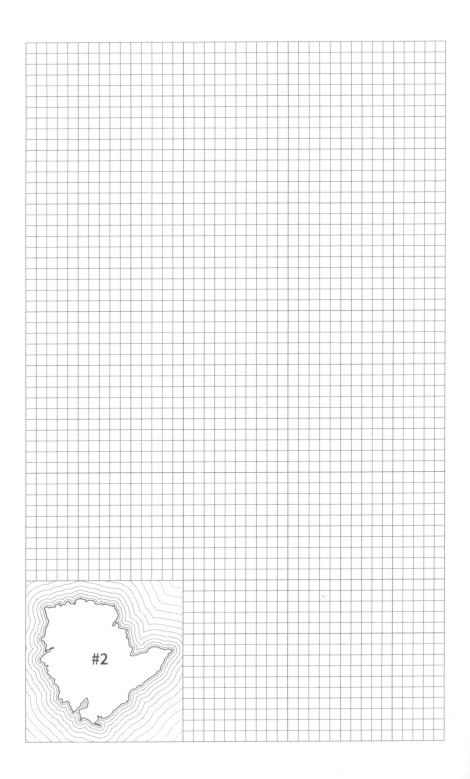

MAP
3

WHO HASN'T FORGOTTEN SOMETHING WHEN ON HOLIDAY?

The map: OS Explorer enlarged to 1:20 000 scale

The story: Kings, cakes and the Somerset Levels

At just 12 metres (39 feet) above sea level, Athelney Hill is barely a lump in the modern landscape. Surrounded by fields and ditches today, over a thousand years ago it was an isolated island hidden in the marsh, mists and shallow waters of the Somerset Levels. Alfred the Great was forced to take refuge on the island after fleeing from the Viking King Guthrum who had attacked Alfred's castle at Chippenham in January 878. It was at this time that Alfred famously burnt the cakes – presumably he had a lot on his plate to think about! He returned in May and defeated Guthrum at the Battle of Edington and, in thanks for his victory, Alfred founded Athelney Abbey in 888. Today only a small monument marks the spot, but in the Middle Ages, along with Glastonbury and Muchelney, the abbey was responsible for much of the drainage that gives us the modern levels. The word 'Rhyne' on the map is a Somerset variation of the old English word for drainage ditch.

◻ Easy

1. Where can you find a triangulation pillar on the map? (Use the key at the front of the book if you're not sure what to look for.)

2. How many well symbols, marked in blue, can you find on this map?

◼ Medium

3. Can you find two places that offer 360° views of the surrounding area? Where are they? One is explicitly labelled; the other can be deduced from the contour lines.

4. Beginning at a farm where it sounds like you might find someone religious, head west along ground of equal height until you reach a road. Following the road in a south-west direction, what is the first historic site you come across?

◼ Tricky

5. Can you find a 'well-spoken' route?

6. Start at a place dedicated to a ninth-century monarch and travel south along the 'musical sound' river until you reach a bridge with a 'catch'. If you head along the footpath, away from the hill, what is the first house you come to?

◼ Challenging

7. On this map, add all of the black spot height numbers together. Refer back to the map of Porth Hellick (page 14) and find the name of a place printed astride an orange contour line that is as many metres high as your total. What is the name of that place?

8. From a confused grubbier word, walk directly to a Taurean path, before turning 90 degrees clockwise and walking to the National Trail. Follow it to your left until you are opposite a utility building. Which one?

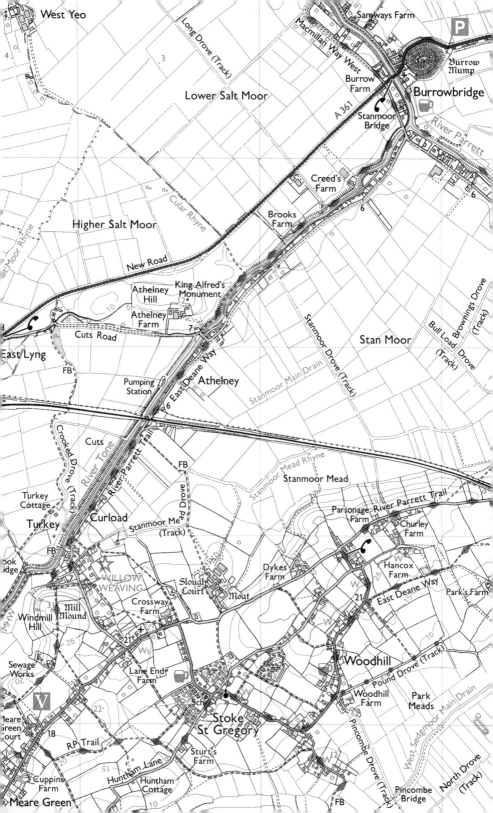

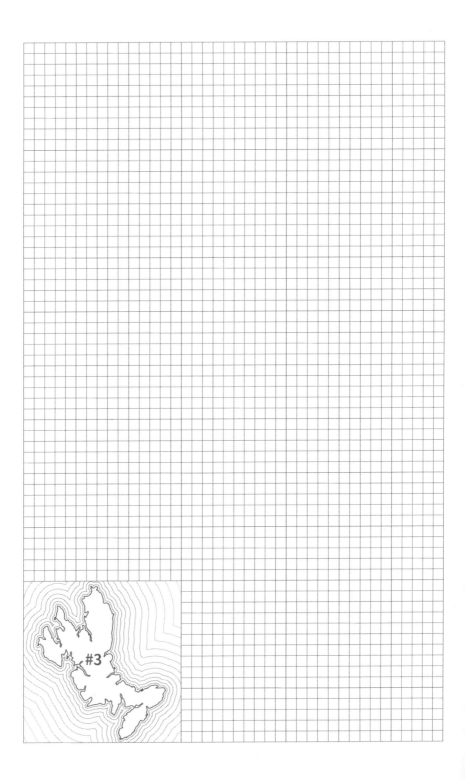

#3

MAP
4

NOT ALWAYS A GRIM PLACE TO LIVE

The map: OS Landranger enlarged to 1:40 000 scale

The story: Grimspound and the Late Bronze Age

The Two Moors Way is a tremendous long-distance path joining the north and south coasts of Devon, taking in the wild open areas of Exmoor and Dartmoor. The section we've chosen here gives you two options: the Webburn Valley or the walk over Hamel Down, which will reward you with an ancient landscape and spectacular views from the exposed weathered outcrops of granite called tors. Around 10,000 years ago, Mesolithic hunter-gatherers began clearing the extensive woodland that covered Dartmoor. By the middle of the Bronze Age it had become farmland and their settlements are the numerous hut circles (roundhouses) marked on the map. Grimspound is one of the best-known examples, believed to date from the Late Bronze Age (about 1450–700 BC) and featuring about 24 huts within a circular stone enclosure. It is not known when Grimspound was abandoned, but the thin moorland soils and climate change, which brought heavy rainfall and reduced soil fertility, eventually made occupation unsustainable, thus producing the landscape we enjoy today.

.

▨ Easy

1. What is the highest height marked on the map?

2. How many farms are labelled on this map?

▨ Medium

3. All around Dartmoor National Park, you can find archaeological structures which are the historic foundations of roundhouses, known as hut circles. How many times does the label 'hut circle', or 'hut circles', appear on the map?

4. Which location on the map needs only one letter changed to become a type of cloud?

▨ Tricky

5. The name of which map location, if you removed its space, would also be found on a London Underground map?

6. What place sounds very much like the coldest season of the year, when spoken out loud?

▨ Challenging

7. Head north from the top of a hill that sounds like a sticky container until you reach an elevation of 370. Walk east until you reach a place of rest, then head due north as the crow flies. How high does that crow have to fly to reach the edge of the map area?

8. Starting at the northernmost of a pair of junctions near a National Trust property:

   a. Head west on what begins as a road and then turns into a public access route, to a road junction that is 74 metres higher than where you started.
   b. Take the road to your left and continue straight until you reach the first turning on your right, then travel across the valley.
   c. Turn right at the crossroads and continue along the road, passing a farm to your left.
   d. Turn right, then left.
   e. Continue straight until you reach a bridleway to your right.
   f. Follow it to a historical embankment.

   What is the name of this landmark?

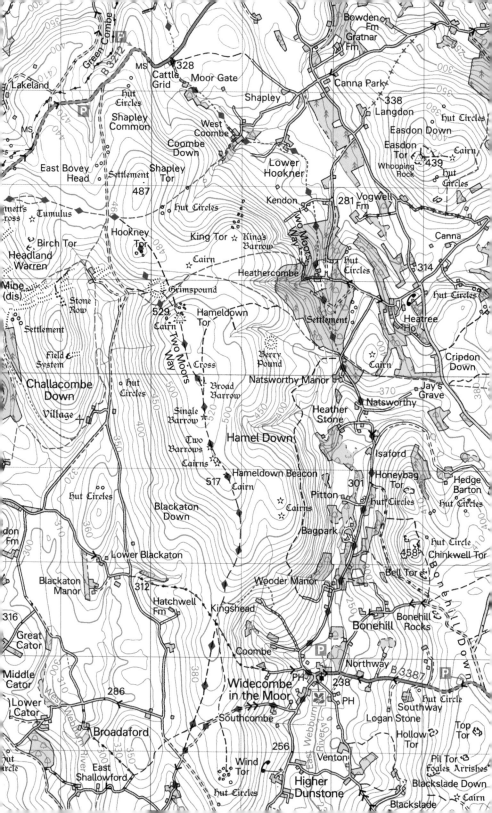

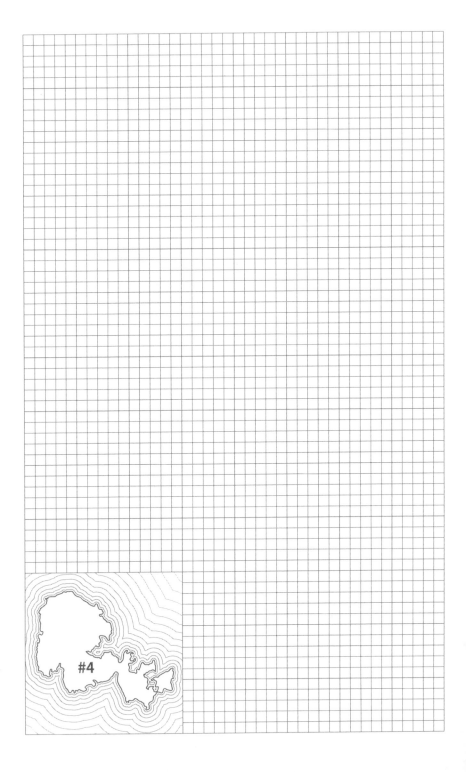

#4

MAP
5

PROBABLY BEST TO SIT THIS ONE OUT

The map: OS Road enlarged to 1:210 000 scale

The story: Cooper's Hill Cheese-Rolling and Wake

Touring Britain today is a lot easier thanks to the great bridges that span our wide estuaries and tidal straits. Before the Severn Bridge was opened in 1966, you had the choice of using a sometimes-hazardous ferry to cross the estuary or a long road journey to the bridge at Gloucester, if you wanted to go across to Wales. But before we leave the South West we'll stop briefly in the Cotswolds and enjoy a little cheese. In the village of Brockworth, a local tradition involves rolling a large Double Gloucester cheese down Cooper's Hill and chasing after it! Originally taking place every Whit Monday as part of a ceremony to maintain grazing rights on the common, the race is now held every Spring Bank Holiday. Watch out for the Master of Ceremonies scattering buns and sweets at the top of the hill, representing the possible pagan origins of the tradition. Injuries are not uncommon so you may want to just take in the views along the Cotswold Way.

▨ Easy

1. If you multiplied the number of nature reserves by the number of buildings of historic interest, both as labelled on the blue map key, what number would result?

2. Which town reportedly gave its name to a well-known racket sport, and where can it be found on the map?

▨ Medium

3. What name on the map, if you delete its final 'e', reads like a tool you might use to groom a lamb?

4. Given that the scale of the map is 1:210,000, how far is it as the crow flies from the answer to question 2 to the Roman Villa, to the nearest kilometre?

▨ Tricky

5. Imagine drawing lines to join the following towns in the order they are given. Each of the four sequences will make the shape of a letter. Taken together, all four letters will complete the name of a butterfly that can be found in the Cotswolds, the _ _ _ _ of Burgundy.

    a. Yate > Cinderford > Chalford > Tetbury > Yate

    b. Upper Soudley > Kingswood > Leighterton > Painswick

    c. Chavenage House > Westonbirt > Long Newnton > Westonbirt > Foxley > Westonbirt > Sherston

    d. Nibley > Frampton Cotterell > Itchington > Bagstone > Itchington > Whitfield > Charfield

6. You may use me to cross an obstacle, but there is not much room to do so. Looking at the map, which location sounds like it could be being described here?

▨ Challenging

7. The following phrases are anagrams of locations on the map. Can you solve them? Each solution uses one fewer space than its corresponding anagram.

    a. TRAINS HOWL   d. BEAT COMES

    b. CORRUPT OLD FONT   e. GROUND HINTS

    c. NORTH RUBY

8. The first letters from each of the answers to the previous question spell out a word, but can you rearrange them to reveal a map location?

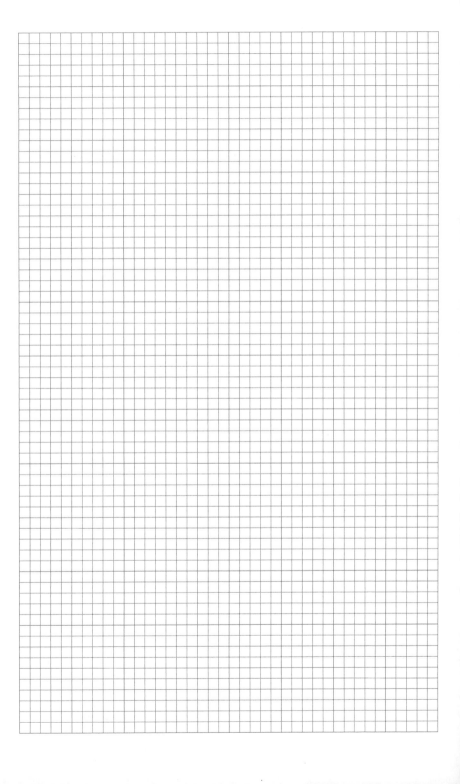

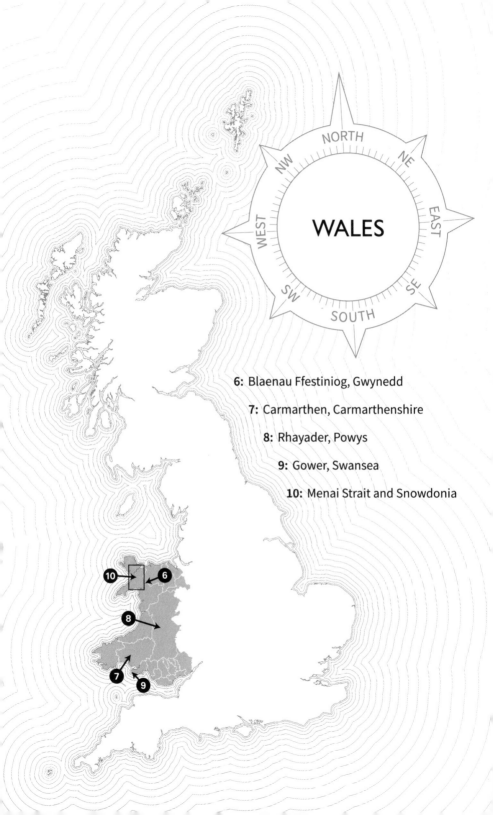

WALES

6: Blaenau Ffestiniog, Gwynedd

7: Carmarthen, Carmarthenshire

8: Rhayader, Powys

9: Gower, Swansea

10: Menai Strait and Snowdonia

GET OUTSIDE!

Name: Jason Rawles

Who are you?

I'm part of the originally selected GetOutside Champion crew. In 2013, I quit IT sales to pursue my passion for adventure and helping people. Ordnance Survey and I have the same values: we want to help people to make positive change and the outdoors is the best place to do that.

In three words, sum up what makes your area the best part of GB

Wales has everything!

Your favourite walk

It has to be a lovely walk over Moel Eilio from Llanberis as it presents some of the best panoramic views in the whole of Great Britain.

Your favourite view

The Lone Tree in Llanberis, north Wales. At sunrise the sun comes up over the Llanberis Pass towards Snowdon, and the reflection off the misty water can be just stunning.

Any local folklore?

Rhitta Gawr is the name of a fearsome giant who used to kill his enemy and then make a cape out of their beards. Rhitta was killed by King Arthur and his body was taken to the summit of Snowdon and covered in stones. Hence how the summit of Snowdon looks!

The perfect day out in your area

I'd start the day with sunrise by the Lone Tree, walk Moel Eilio over lunch and then finish the day with a walk on Newborough Beach to see the sunset. Two of those are based from Llanberis and the beach is a very short drive away.

Why people should visit

Because the area has something for everyone. It's accessible, adventurous and a wonderful playground for all – the perfect place to GetOutside!

MAP
6

ROOFING THE WORLD

The map: OS Six Inch 1899 (hand tinted)

The story: Slate mining

Although described as quarries on the map, the Oakeley and Llechwedd slate quarries were actually mines, with Oakeley the largest in the world when it was in use. The impact of this industrial effort changed vast expanses of the landscape, which today makes the area distinctive and even attractive in its own way. By the end of the 18th century, Wales was producing over 26,000 tons of slate, dominating the rest of the UK's workings until the government imposed a 20 per cent tax on all slate carried around the coast. This advantaged those that could use the inland canals in England. Slate sent overseas, however, wasn't taxed and exports to the United States increased. Ffestiniog quarry supplied much of the roofing slate needed by Germany after fire destroyed large parts of Hamburg in 1842. The tax was abolished in 1831 and slate production peaked through the middle of the 19th century, helped by development of the railways.

QUESTIONS

■ Easy

1. How many aqueducts can you find on the map?

2. Which European country's name appears on the map?

■ Medium

3. Which two locations on the map share their name with a northern sea of the Atlantic Ocean?

4. What street name becomes a legendary animal with the addition of an 'i'?

■ Tricky

5. What abbreviation on the map is also an informal way of saying 'man'? How many times can you find this exact abbreviation on the map?

6. What is the distance, as the crow flies, from the hospital to the county school? And what is the shortest distance from the most easterly pub to the Barlwyd river?

■ Challenging

7. Start at the most northerly, still body of water on the map. Travel south until you reach a tramway, then east until you reach the river. Follow the path of the river in a northerly direction until you reach a benchmark number where the second and third digit add up to the first. Travel north along the main road next to this number until you reach a named building. What is it?

8. Can you use words on the map to solve the following cryptic crossword clues?

   a. Cascade after wall tumbled
   b. Slope in 151 points

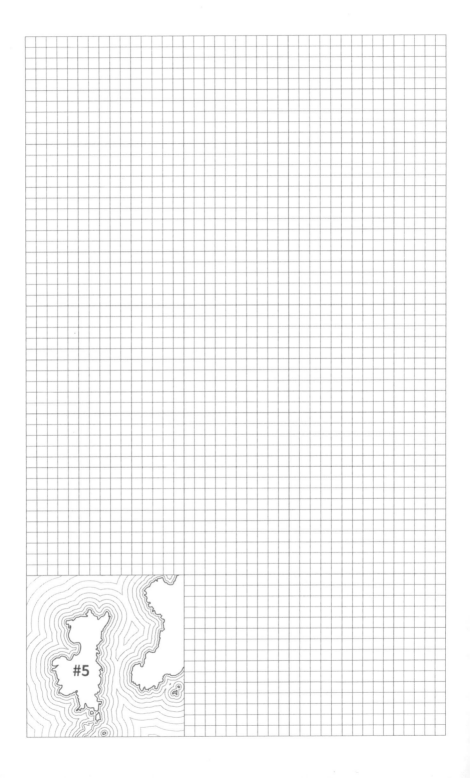

MAP
7

LOCATION, LOCATION, LOCATION

The map: Open Map Local Vector at 1:8 000 scale

The story: Scratching the surface of this ancient historic capital

Carmarthen's pre-Roman origins make it one of the oldest towns in Wales – if not the oldest. It was the civitas capital of the Demetae tribe and known as Moridunum (or 'sea fort'), commanding a defensive elevated position on the River Towy about 18 km (11 miles) from the sea. It remained one of the most populous towns in Wales until the Industrial Revolution and the rapid development of the South Wales coalfields. Known in medieval times as the town of St Teulyddog's (Llanteulyddog), its first Norman castle was destroyed by Llywelyn the Great in 1215. The castle was rebuilt by 1223 and walls were added that helped secure the town for almost 200 years until it was plundered by Owain Glyndwr in 1405. The Black Book of Carmarthen – which is named after the colour of its binding and its connection with the local priory – is the earliest surviving Welsh-language book. It dates from around 1250 and mentions the legend of King Arthur.

▨ Easy

1. How many times can you find the word 'Morgan' on the map?

2. Can you find three identical blue symbols that align so that you could draw a straight line through the exact centre of all three?

▨ Medium

3. Where on this map would you find the name of a small, rounded boat?

4. Which location on this map sounds like a pleased road surface?

▨ Tricky

5. If you remove an 'R' and an 'E' from the name of a certain street, which famous 1980s videogame remains?

6. There are two streets that have 'smaller' versions of themselves on the map. What are they?

▨ Challenging

7. What is the fewest number of left turns you could take to get from the most southerly car park to the most northerly church with a tower, assuming the church entrance faces north?

8. Find three parallel roads that share a three-letter word. Heading out from the middle of these roads, turn right, then left onto a road that sounds like it might smell like hops. Take the sixth right, then the first left, passing a place of worship on your right. If you turn right, which building is labelled at the first four-way junction you reach?

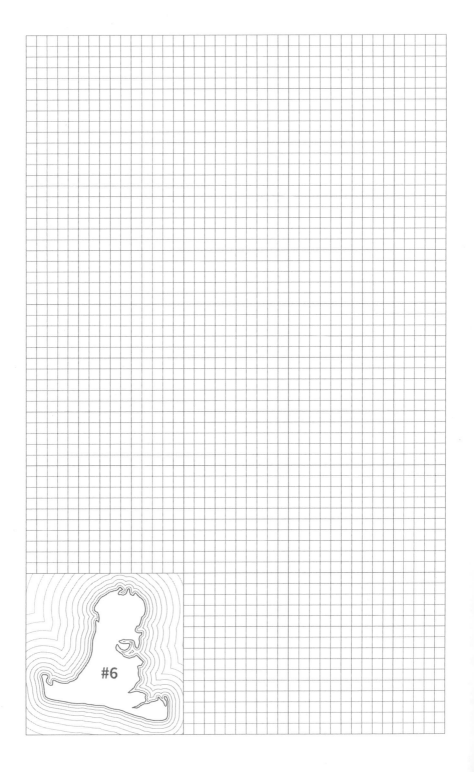

#6

MAP
8

CRISS-CROSSING HISTORY

The map: OS Explorer enlarged to 1:20 000 scale

The story: Rebecca, what hairy legs you have

The easiest routes through mountains, taking advantage of river valleys and straightforward crossing points, often encourage settlements such as Rhayader in mid-Wales. The Romans forded the river here on their way to their lead and silver mines, but it was the battles between the Norman Marcher Lords and the Welsh princes in the 12th century that caused the first castle to be built to control access up river. Rhayader developed into a market town serving the surrounding rural area, with mills and a market hall at the centre crossroads. During the 18th and 19th centuries, turnpike trusts were set up to improve the main roads, collecting tolls and controlling access. In Rhayader, the burden of this extra cost led impoverished local farmers to riot and three tollgates were demolished on 11 October 1843. Dressed as women and known as 'Rebeccaites', the men returned on 2 November to destroy the North, East and Rhayader Bridge gates. Most of their grievances were addressed after a Commission of Inquiry took place, but it wasn't the last time the 'Rebecca' tactic was used.

▨ Easy

1. How many quarries are marked on the map?

2. Which two leisure activities are available within 250 metres of Weirglodd?

▧ Medium

3. Which type of ancient feature on this map can you also find on the map of Dartmoor (see page 27)?

4. Which short word on the map is a noun that becomes an appropriate verb when reversed?

▩ Tricky

5. Start at the junction of the Wye river and its largest pictured tributary.
   a. Go north-east along the river until you reach a bridge labelled to your right.
   b. Go under the bridge, staying on the smaller stream, and pass under another labelled bridge.
   c. The brook will split off into two directions; take the stream that goes north, bearing left when it splits again.
   d. Continue until you reach a footpath running perpendicular to the path of the brook.
   e. Break away from the river to follow the path until you reach a road, then head in a northerly direction along the road until you can rejoin the footpath. Continuing along that footpath, what is the first landmark you reach?

6. Where might a breezy toy go if it was hungry?

▩ Challenging

7. What place on the map contains within it a word that means 'used up carelessly'?

8. Start at the Nature Reserve and travel uphill until you reach the highest point on the map. Head south to a place where you could cross a river without a bridge. If you walked west through a forest, what is the first road you would come to?

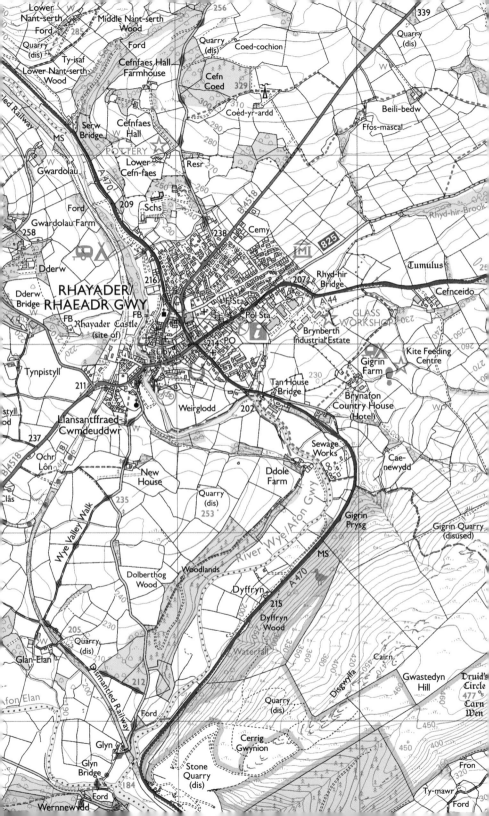

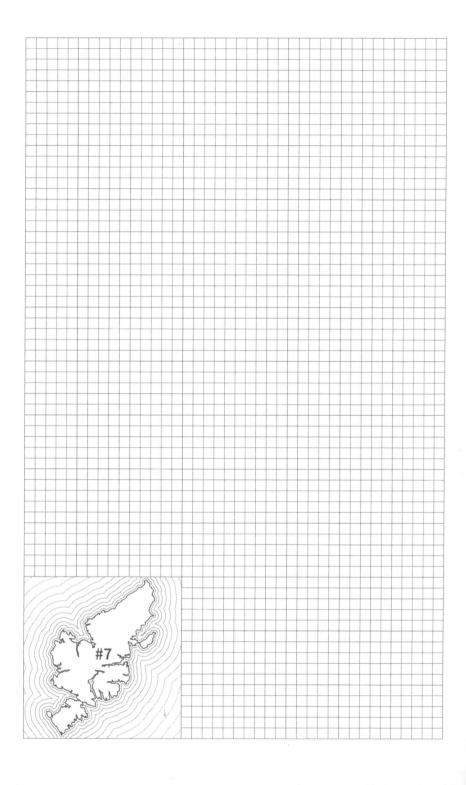

MAP
9

THE BEACH WASN'T ALWAYS THIS CLOSE

The map: OS Landranger enlarged to 1:40 000 scale

The story: Paviland Cave and the Ice Age

A walk along the 1,400-km (870-mile) Wales Coast Path will bring you to Rhossili Bay, one of the best beaches in Wales (some say the world). Ideally placed at the western end of the Gower Peninsula it is part of the very first Area of Outstanding Natural Beauty in the UK, designated in 1956. The caves in the Gower's limestone cliffs preserve evidence of the earliest human occupation in Wales. Paviland Cave in particular has provided important understanding of the Early Upper Palaeolithic period in Britain at the end of the last Ice Age. At this time the Gower would have been an elevated plateau and the cave a long way from the sea due to the lower sea level. The burial chambers on the map are from the Neolithic period (c. 4000 to c. 2000 BC) and the promontory forts and defended hilltops indicate occupation from prehistory into early medieval times.

Easy

1. How many words on the map begin with a double-'L'?

2. How many different colours can you find within the names of places on the map?

Medium

3. Connect all four triangulation points with straight lines to form a quadrilateral shape. The land of how many National Trust sites can be found within the boundaries of this shape?

4. How many different religious and/or royal titles can you find on the map, either as single words or as the start of a word?

Tricky

5. Starting at the most southerly 51 metre spot height shown on the map, travel south until you find another spot height 2 metres lower than the first. Once there, travel south-west to a place which could also be a 'scoundrel'. Take the closest National Trail south-eastward until you reach the last named point on that path. Can you find another location on the map that shares the same first word as that point?

6. Can you find locations on the map that are anagrams of the following words or phrases? Ignore the spaces and punctuation, which may differ from those in the place names.
   a. MEMORY KILO   b. CRUEL HOVEL   c. RETAIN POTS

Challenging

7. Can you find a two-word location, expanding the abbreviated part marked on the map, that sounds like a trivial observation?

8. From the National Trust location with limited access, travel uphill to the nearest triangulation pillar. Follow the bridleway just to its east, heading northwards past another National Trust property until you reach a place that sounds like the site of a blaze. Travel due east from there until you reach the rightmost edge of the quadrilateral from question 3. Heading due south from here, which is the first marked settlement you come to?

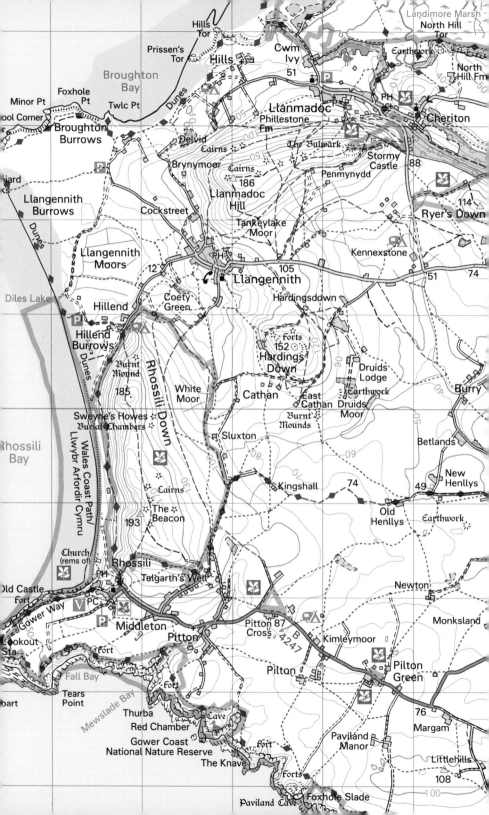

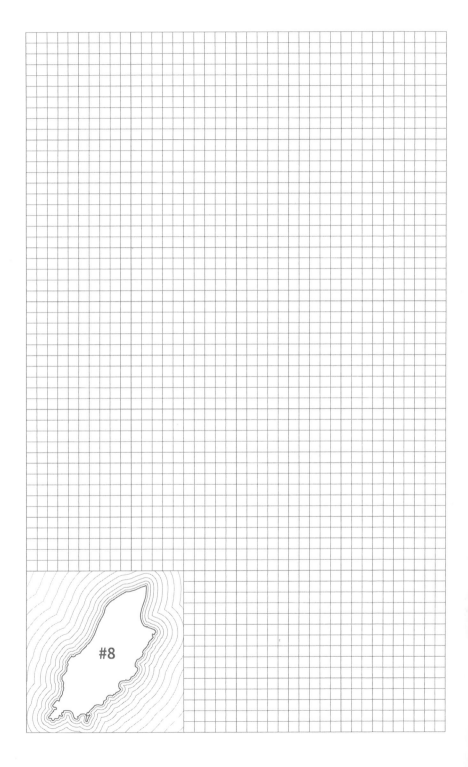

#8

MAP
10

DID YOU FEEL THE GROUND SHAKE?

The map: OS Road enlarged to 1:210 000 scale

The story: Bridging the Menai Strait

The narrow strait that separates Anglesey from the rest of North Wales was formed by rising sea levels after the last period of glaciation around 22,000 years ago. The rocks of the island are geologically distinct from those that make up Snowdonia – a major fault line runs under the strait and is the most seismically active area in Wales. The Wales Coast Path is an ideal way to explore both the landscape and history of the area, especially if you want to see the impressive bridges that span the two shorelines. The Menai Suspension Bridge (A5 road) in particular is still considered one of the great industrial achievements of the 19th century. The bridge had to allow 100-metre clearance for the tall ships, commercial and naval, that used the strait as a short cut. To keep the shipping lane open, the bridge needed to be built without scaffolding, further adding to the challenge of its construction.

◼ Easy

1. Given that the Welsh for river is 'Afon', how many rivers are named on the map?

2. How many 'camping and caravan site' symbols can you find on the map?

◼ Medium

3. Which location sounds like somewhere a person from the Netherlands could store his money?

4. If you add an 'a', which map location becomes the name of a soft toffee?

◼ Tricky

5. Starting on the peak of a hill that is 734 metres tall, if you were to travel in a straight line to a peak that is 78 metres taller, how many roads would you cross over?

6. By changing just one letter in a word on the map, can you find a significant Biblical New Testament location?

◼ Challenging

7. Can you find three locations on the map in which the entire labelled place name contains no vowels whatsoever?

8. What is the distance (to the nearest half-kilometre) from the site of a 1461 battle to the highest point on the map?

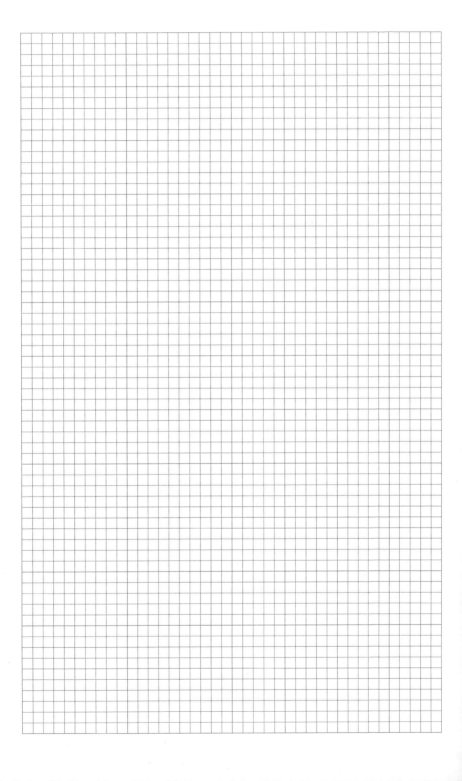

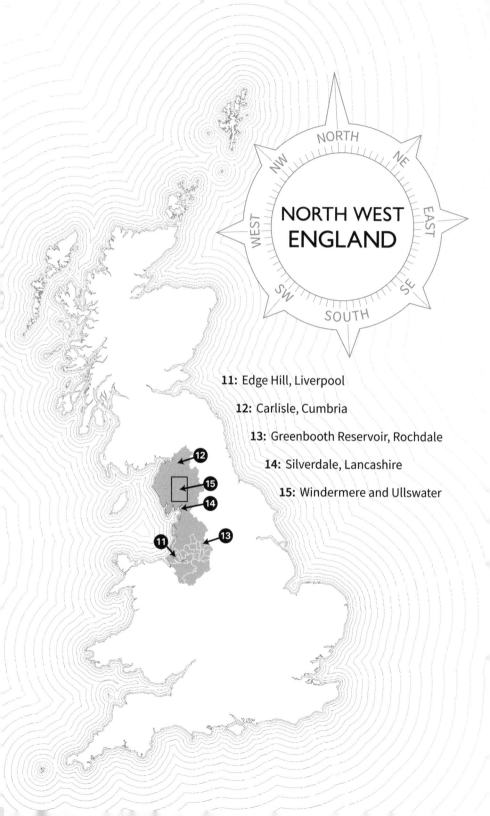

NORTH WEST
ENGLAND

11: Edge Hill, Liverpool

12: Carlisle, Cumbria

13: Greenbooth Reservoir, Rochdale

14: Silverdale, Lancashire

15: Windermere and Ullswater

GET OUTSIDE!

Name: James Forrest

Who are you?

I'm James Forrest, a.k.a. Mountain Man, as the Sunday Telegraph nicknamed me. I'm a record-breaking adventurer known for climbing all 446 mountains in England and Wales in just six months – the fastest-ever time.

In three words, sum up what makes your area the best part of GB

Mountains, lakes, people.

Your favourite walk

It was the first mountain I ever climbed, aged eight, with my family and it was the hill that hooked me on the great outdoors and led to a lifelong love of climbing mountains. It has to be Cat Bells – that classic little Lakeland climb that serves up enough drama to make you feel like an adventurer, even if you've only got an hour or two to spend in the fells.

Your favourite view

The panorama over Crummock Water from the summit of Low Fell. It's a view that never ceases to take my breath away.

Any local folklore?

An eachy is the name given to a gruesome species of lake monster reportedly seen in the waters of Windermere and Bassenthwaite.

The perfect day out in your area

I'd start with fresh coffee in a Cockermouth café and a gentle stroll around quaint Loweswater, before treating myself to lunch at the charming Kirkstile Inn. Next I'd climb up Red Pike, hike along the Buttermere Edge ridge and then wild camp under the stars on Haystacks. Perfection.

Why people should visit

From the vibrant cities of Liverpool and Manchester to the wild, remote mountains of the Lake District, there is something for everyone in the North West.

MAP
11

ALL CHANGE AT EDGE HILL

The map: OS 25-inch 1905 (hand tinted)

The story: The oldest working railway station in the world

The first Edge Hill station in Liverpool opened on the Liverpool and Manchester Railway in 1830 in a narrow cutting to the west of the current station. From there, inclines to the docks and the passenger terminal at Crown Street were used to complete the journey as locomotives were forbidden in the tunnels. Within months, directors of the railway decided that they needed a station much closer to the city centre and George Stephenson drew up plans for a new station at the portals of two new tunnels to the docks and passenger terminal at Lime Street. The new Edge Hill station opened in 1836 and continued the practice of rolling trains into Lime Street by gravity and hauling them back using winding engines until 1870. The station remains in use today, although almost everything else on this map besides the main through roads and railway lines have been redeveloped.

Easy

1. Which two streets share their names with a Nordic country and its capital?

2. How many pubs, marked 'P.H.', can you find on the map?

Medium

3. Which street has a name that implies a connection to plants?

4. What is the total number of weighing machines further south than the centre of Ryder Street?

Tricky

5. How many buildings would the 'bird' labelled on the map fly over if it travelled straight to the eastern triangulation point.

6. Start where a street that shares its first name with a London Underground station meets some tramlines, then travel east until you have passed three pubs. Take the first left, turn left again at the end of the road, then take the first road on the right. How many houses face west on this street?

Challenging

7. The first words of which two street names from the map are combined in the anagram PENNY WEEKS?

8. Subtract twice the number of signal points from the number of the benchmark with the highest elevation. Where is the benchmark that matches your answer?

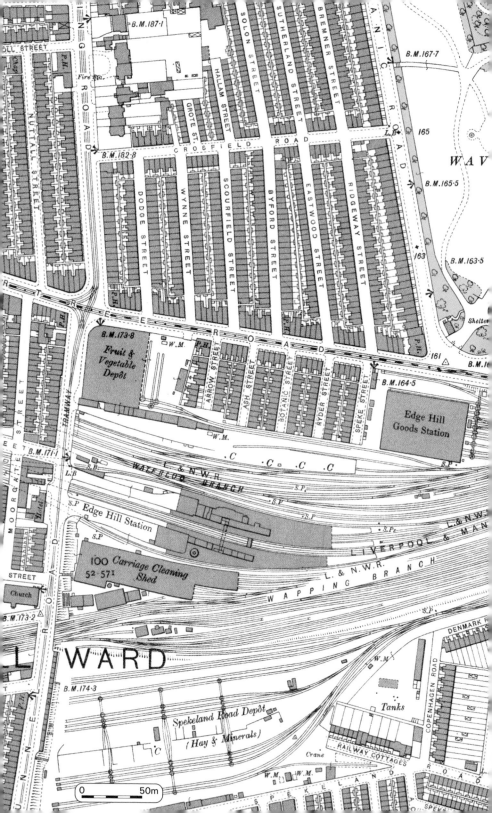

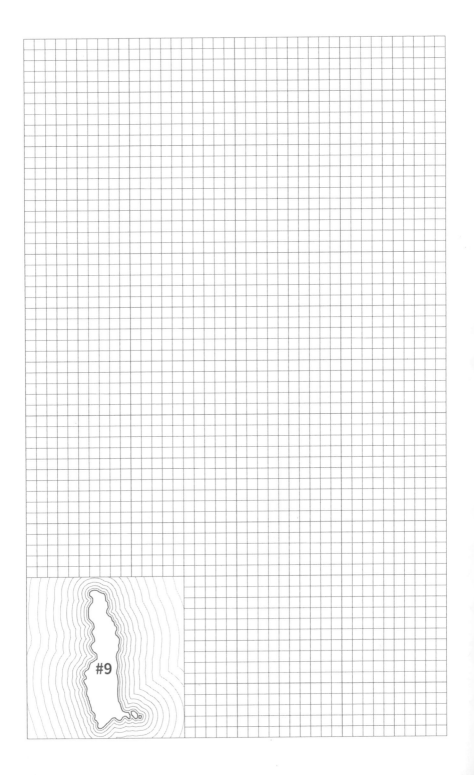

#9

MAP
12

TWO A PENNY

The map: Open Map Local Vector at 1:8 000 scale

The story: Market towns

Market towns developed in the Middle Ages to service the needs of a growing population and an economy that was increasingly becoming cash-based. The first market towns developed near castles and monasteries, not just because of the protection they offered, but also to meet their demand for supplies and services. From there, they grew to serve surrounding villages and farms, often where roads crossed a river, becoming a focal point for the area. Many marketplaces featured a stone cross, with steps and roofs added to some, giving rise to the buttercross, where dairy produce could be kept cool. Although markets were often held in a large open area called the Market Square, most were not that shape. The right to hold weekly markets was granted by royal charter and in 1352 King Edward III also granted Carlisle the right to hold an annual August fair. These 'super' markets drew visitors from across Cumbria and were important social events. Markets also generated money that could be put into improving a town's defences, important for places like Carlisle near the border of Scotland.

Easy

1. Can you find ten streets with boys' names in?

2. Can you locate a triangle of three roads, plus a short unnamed road above them, that form the shape of a clothes hanger?

Medium

3. At how many places shown on the map could you drive across a watercourse?

4. If the scale of the map is 1: 8 000, how far is it from the bus station to the most northerly museum? Give your answer to the nearest 100 metres, as the crow flies.

Tricky

5. Can you find 'an argument within a fortress'?

6. Can you identify two place names that each appear in two different road names?

Challenging

7. Excluding Carlisle itself, how many English cities can you find named on the map?

8. Start from a slippery place, and leap the barrier to the insect park. Cross an original flower to play a set. Write out the initials of these five places in the order visited, then take the fourth, eighth and ninth letters. What are you now?

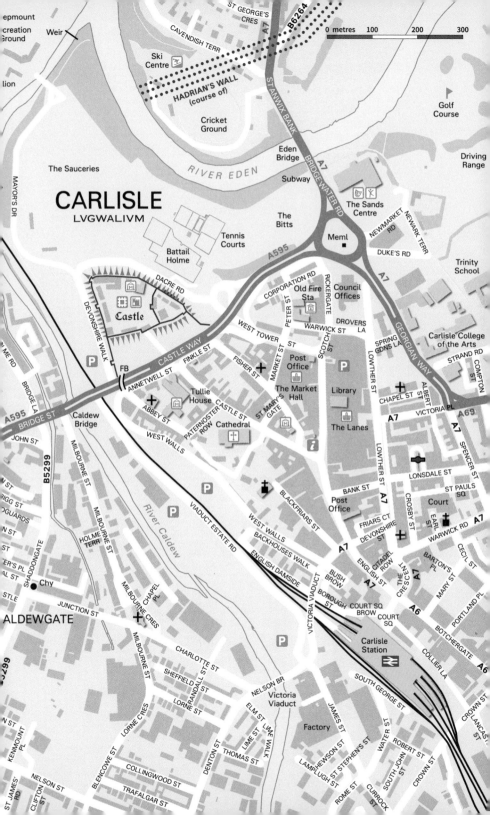

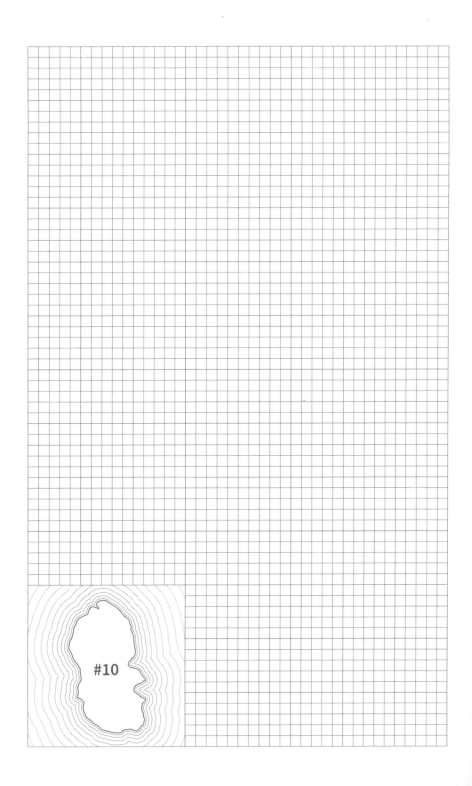

#10

MAP
13

DAM THAT WATER

The map: OS Explorer enlarged to 1:20 000 scale

The story: Reservoirs? More needed!

Our need for better and faster communication links, cleaner energy and additional fresh water continues to reshape and rework the landscape. Here, in the hills above Rochdale, the edges of disued quarries of past industries soften into the hillside while modern wind turbines spring up tall against the skyline. The expanding towns and cities of the Industrial Revolution not only obliterated rural farmland, but also drove the need for large reservoirs. The three Naden reservoirs were completed in 1846 against objections from the mill owners in the valley below. Demand continued to grow, leading the water company to add Greenbooth reservoir in the 1960s, submerging the mill and village after which it is named. There are plans for new reservoirs today, with landscapes captured by our maps before and after they change.

▓ Easy

1. How many wind turbines are marked on the map? And how many masts?

2. Which place shares its name with an active volcano in Sicily?

▓ Medium

3. Where might you quarry some 'feline' rocks?

4. Can you find a place whose name could crudely describe an ancient grave?

▓ Tricky

5. Where on the map sounds like a small sound?

6. Which location on the map sounds like a synonym for 'simple but cosy' when its word order is reversed?

▓ Challenging

7. If you were to draw a path connecting these locations in order, what letter would you draw?
   a. The most southerly farm
   b. The most westerly triangulation pillar
   c. A place which is an anagram of HARE IRONS
   d. Somewhere that sounds like part of a fish's face
   e. A place where you might keep your money safe

8. Find a black spot height that matches an orange contour height. Imagine a line through their centres that extends on both sides to the edge of the map. From where that line enters water, travel due south to the first farm you find, then exactly northwest until you reach the edge of a reservoir. Travel north along the shore until you reach a brook. Following the direction of the brook, heading away from the reservoir, which is the first labelled feature that you reach?

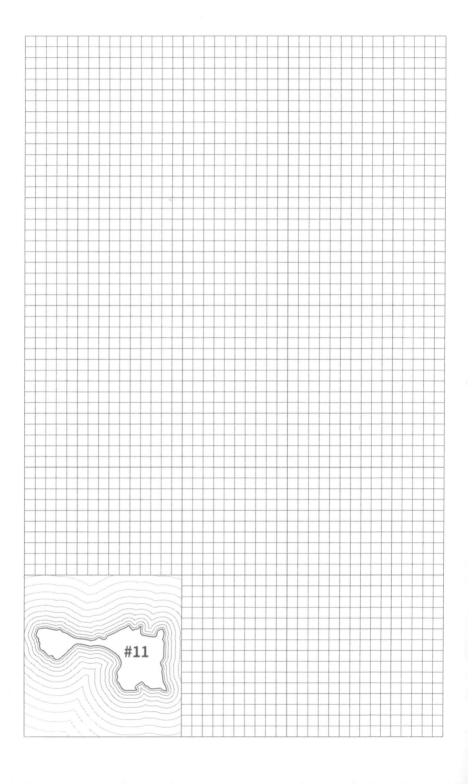

#11

MAP

14

DON'T RUSH BY ON THE M6

The map: OS Landranger enlarged to 1:40 000 scale

The story: Warton Crag

The Arnside and Silverdale Area of Outstanding Natural Beauty (AONB) is a small but remarkable area with rare and distinctive wildlife that thrives amongst its marshes, wooded hills and exposed limestone crags. The highest point in the AONB is Warton Crag, its carboniferous limestone layers exposed during the last Ice Age and then sculpted by rainwater to create the distinctive blocks (clints) and deep cracks (grykes) we see today. More extensive areas of limestone pavement exist to the east, but Warton rewards you with some great coastal views and the convenience of a railway station at Carnforth. The summit of Warton Crag, appearing defensive in nature, was originally thought to be a fort. However, more recent archaeological work suggests it was a Bronze Age enclosure with more peaceful intent.

Easy

1. How many level crossings appear on this map?
2. How many nature reserves could you visit that are further north than Silverdale?

Medium

3. What colour connects a 'bridge' with the 'hills'?
4. Can you find two places that include a word for a pigeon shelter in their name?

Tricky

5. What are John, Robert and Ted Kennedy? Can you find a place on the map that answers this question?
6. Which places could these phrases refer to?
   a. A lazy school leader
   b. A place where a magical being might ascend

Challenging

7. How far is it, as the crow flies, from the highest point marked on the map to the viewpoint, considering the scale of the map is 1:40 000? Give your answer to the nearest kilometre.

8. Starting at Arnside train station, take a southbound train and get off at the next stop. Stepping onto the road directly outside of the station, turn left and continue on this road past three junctions. At the next junction, keep following the on-road cycle route, then turn right at the end, and keep going until you reach the National Trail. If you follow the trail east, ignoring a first turning to the left, what is the first labelled place you will reach?

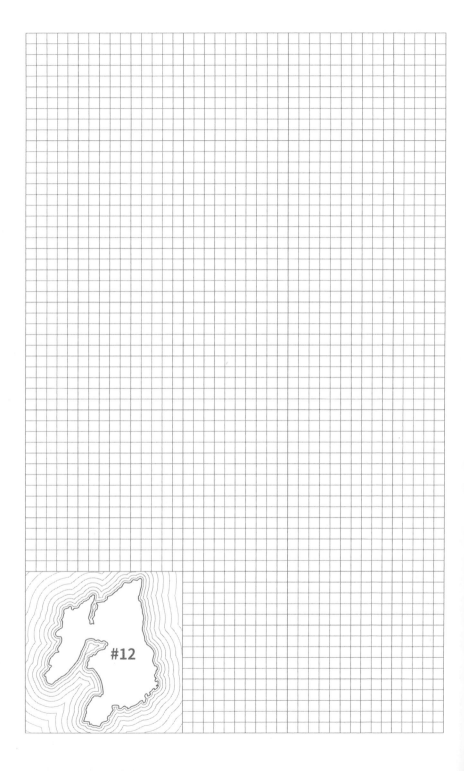

#12

MAP
15

NO COFFEE SHOPS ON THIS HIGH STREET

The map: OS Road enlarged to 1:210 000 scale

The story: Crossing the fells

It would be true to say that the Romans generally built straight roads, but even they couldn't ignore tricky terrain and would take an easier or safer route if it served them. When they started to push north, around 70 AD, they had to tackle the wilder and more mountainous parts of Britain, although the warmer climate of this period would have made building a road along the top of the Cumbrian mountains a more attractive prospect than tackling the densely wooded valleys. An ancient trackway is thought to have already existed over the fells between Windermere and the Eden Valley when the Romans looked to link their forts at Galava (Ambleside) and Brocavum (Brougham) near Penrith. Taking in the highest point in the Eastern fells, you can still see remnants of the Roman road which gave this fell its 'High Street' name.

▨ Easy

1. Where on the map sounds like somewhere suitable to go shopping?

2. Where can you find the name 'Hutton' in three different locations on the map?

▨ Medium

3. Which location sounds like it is likely to commit a crime?

4. Which feature on the map is only one letter different to a very similar feature on the previous map?

▨ Tricky

5. What location on the map is the name of a sea-dwelling animal that lacks a common feature of many sea-dwelling animals that can itself be found as another location on the map?

6. Follow the River Kent north from the bottom of the map until you reach a named reservoir. Ascend to the highest point within 1 km. Travel north-west to a peak that is 195 metres higher than your current position, then travel east as the crow flies until you reach a place of worship. Where are you?

▨ Challenging

7. Count the number of public telephone symbols within the boundary formed by the A591, the A6 and the A66, then add this to the second-lowest spot height number on the map. Add the number of camping sites where you can also park a caravan, anywhere on the map, to the total. Rearrange the digits of the resulting number to find a spot height on the map. What is that spot height?

8. Can you find words on the map that can be broken down into multiple words with the following meanings?

   a. Question pork
   b. Deer concession
   c. Spoil valley
   d. Moor beam

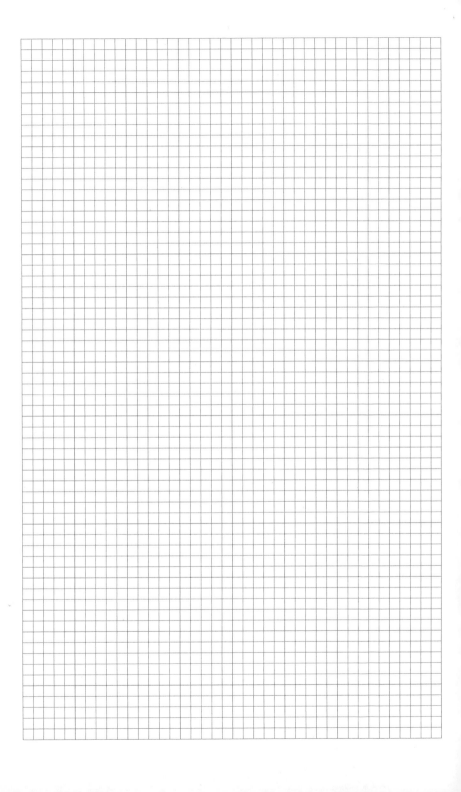

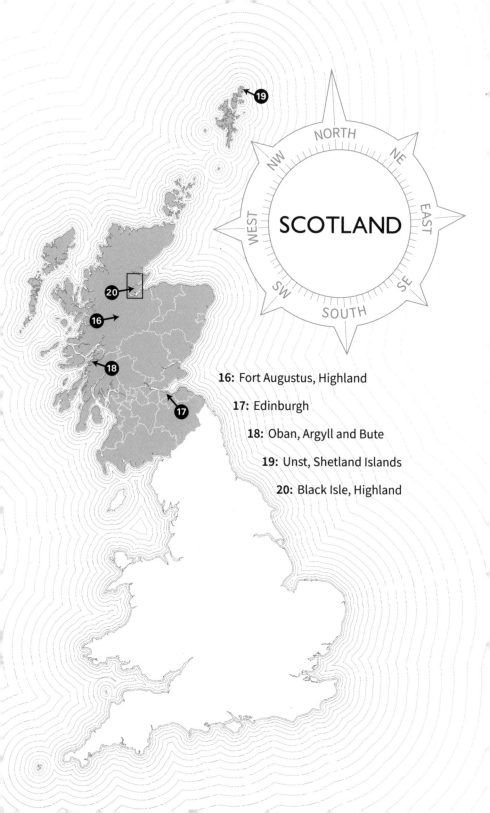

SCOTLAND

NORTH
NE
EAST
SE
SOUTH
SW
WEST
NW

16: Fort Augustus, Highland

17: Edinburgh

18: Oban, Argyll and Bute

19: Unst, Shetland Islands

20: Black Isle, Highland

GET OUTSIDE!

Name: Cat Webster

Who are you?
I'm a hillwalker, skier, wild camper, a qualified mountain leader and a volunteer walk leader.

In three words, sum up what makes your area the best part of GB
Mountains, glens, lochs!

Your favourite walk
It's hard to choose, but one is Meall a' Bhuachaille, a Corbett near Aviemore in the Highlands. It takes in remnants of ancient Caledonian pine, a green lochan – which legend tells got its striking colour from fairies washing their clothes – a bothy and fantastic views of the Cairngorms.

Your favourite view
It's hard to beat the impressive sight of Buachaille Etive Mòr rising out of Rannoch Moor at the entrance to Glen Coe. It's the absolute classic Scottish view.

Any local folklore?
Am Fear Liath Mòr – the Big Grey Man of Ben MacDui – is said to haunt the second highest mountain in the UK, with tales of hikers experiencing a strange presence or uncontrollable fear at the summit and hearing crunching footsteps in the mist . . .

The perfect day out
My perfect day would start from a wild camp in a remote glen with the smell of fresh coffee brewing on the stove. A long day of ridge walking and scrambling in the sunshine would be followed by a dip in a mountain pool and then I'd watch the sun go down with a beer and some fish and chips at the nearest pub – bliss!

Why people should visit
I'm biased of course but I really do think that with its mountains, glens, lochs and beaches, Scotland has some of the most stunning scenery, not just in Great Britain but in the world!

MAP
16

DEEP WATERS

The map: OS 25-inch 1899 (hand tinted)

The story: Great Glen and the Caledonian Canal

The Great Glen divides the north-west Highlands of Scotland from the Grampian Mountains to the south-east and provides a natural path between Fort William and Inverness. The associated fault line contributes to the very deep waters of Loch Ness, which holds the largest volume of fresh water in the British Isles. The natural corridor of the glen led to plans in the 18th century to link up its lochs with a canal, but they were shelved over concerns about strong winds in the lochs channelled between the mountains. The idea was revived in 1773 to support the struggling fishing industry and engineer James Watt was commissioned to survey a route, but it wasn't until 1803 that construction was finally approved, amid growing concerns over the depressed economy, unemployment and the Highland Clearances. Work began from both ends so that the canal could be used as it was built to transport equipment and materials into the Great Glen. The project ran 12 years over schedule and cost twice as much as planned and by the time it opened steam ships had reduced the problem of sailing stormy coastal waters and were too big for the canal. Today it remains popular as one of the most scenic waterways in the world, supporting the local economy in ways never imagined by its designers.

▥ Easy

1. How many bridges are marked on the map?

2. How many times are mooring posts indicated on the map? Some are abbreviated.

▥ Medium

3. The larger black numbers on the map are field numbers. If you add the highest field number north of the River Oich to the highest number south of the same river, what number results?

4. Can you find three locations on the map where you might expect to find members of the clergy living?

▥ Tricky

5. Which place on the map, if you added a letter, would describe a water-related levy?

6. Start on the footpath in Bunoich with the well immediately to your left. Follow the path until you reach a road, then turn left. Walk past a place where you might have found an anvil, then continue along the road and cross the river. Follow the path in a direction that will allow you to pass by both coniferous and non-coniferous trees on your right. As you continue to follow the path, what is the first building complex on your right?

▥ Challenging

7. Using the map legend, estimate how long it would take you to walk from The Lodge to the Post Office if you walked at a constant speed of 5 km/h.

8. Each of the following lines contains a jumble of the letters from two map labels. Can you solve each mixed anagram to reveal the two original labels?
   a. PILE ROCKS
   b. THE SOLO LOCH
   c. VISITOR PINNACLE
   d. ABOUT SANE HOMES

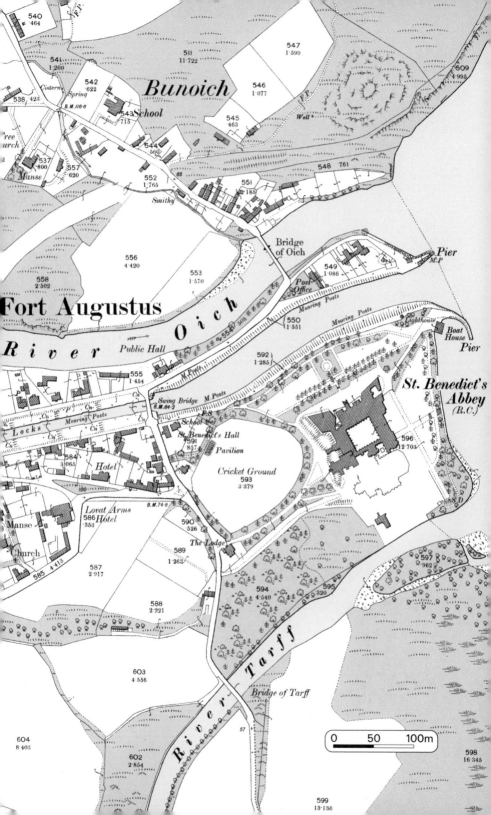

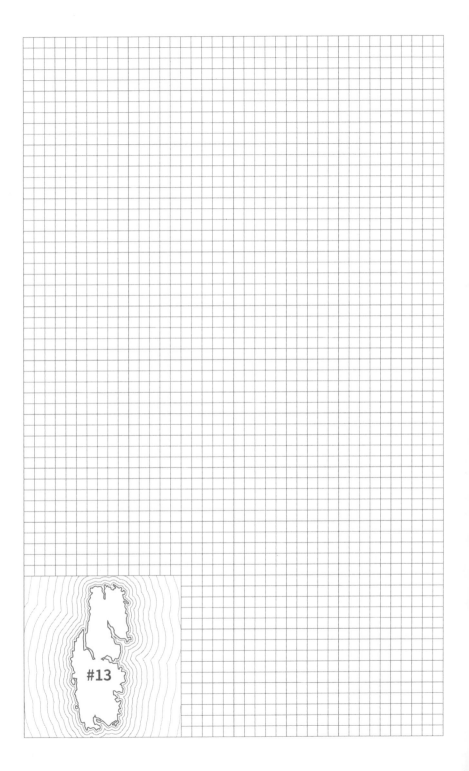

#13

MAP

17

LOOK OUT BELOW!

The map: Open Map Local Vector at 1:8 000 scale

The story: Edinburgh's Old and New Town

Edinburgh grew rapidly in the 16th century and overcrowding became an increasing problem within the defensive wall that was built after the Battle of Flodden Field in 1513. The solution was to build upwards, with some properties reaching 12 stories high. Such was the need for living space within the Old Town that on top of these stone-built buildings wooden houses were added. This continued into the 17th century and the overcrowding, lack of clean water and open sewers meant disease and plague were ever-present. Navigating the narrow medieval streets around the Royal Mile (High Street on the map) would have also, meant facing the added hazard of residents from the upper floors shouting 'Gardyloo!' and emptying their washing water or chamber pots from the windows above. Daniel Defoe, author of *Robinson Crusoe*, remarked that 'in no city in the world [do] so many people live in so little room as at Edinburgh'. The need for the wall declined after the union with England in 1707 and plans to expand the city began in 1752. A little-known young architect, James Craig, won the competition to design a 'New Town' and laid out the large parallel streets, squares and gardens north of Princes Street that today give Edinburgh its distinctive character.

▦ Easy

1. Which word features more on the map: North or South? (Don't count the abbreviations 'N' or 'S'.)

2. How many museums and art galleries are marked on the map?

▦ Medium

3. Can you find six place names with age-related words in their titles, such as 'old'?

4. Can you identify two different street names on the map that imply you might find turf for sale at their locations?

▦ Tricky

5. If the scale of the map is 1:8 000, how far is it as the crow flies from the most northerly church with a spire to a leisure location with a name that suggests pandemonium? Give your answer to the nearest 100 metres.

6. Can you find a location that would be named after a British city, were it to have one extra letter added to its end?

▦ Challenging

7. Can you identify a route from Chalmers Street to Castlehill that requires only travelling on three other differently named streets en route? For the purpose of this question, don't count a street towards your total if you only cross directly over it, without travelling along it.

8. From a city in Lower Saxony, travel through Scotland's national flower to a Welsh saint. Passing by royalty to Jorvik, what place do you come to?

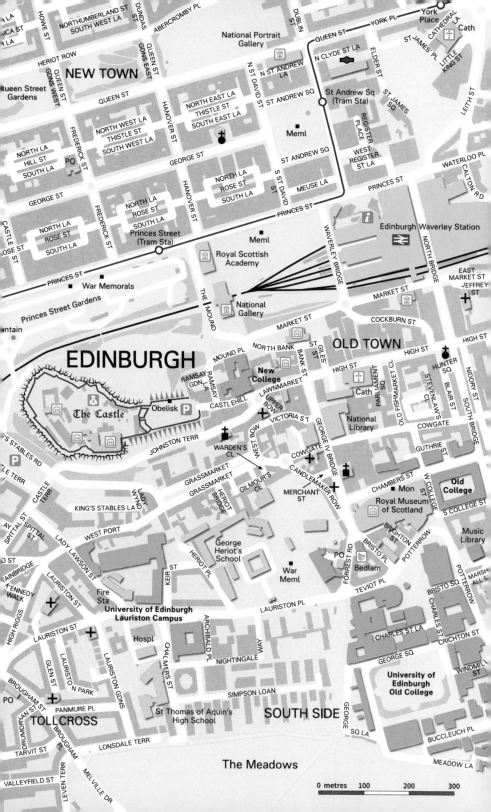

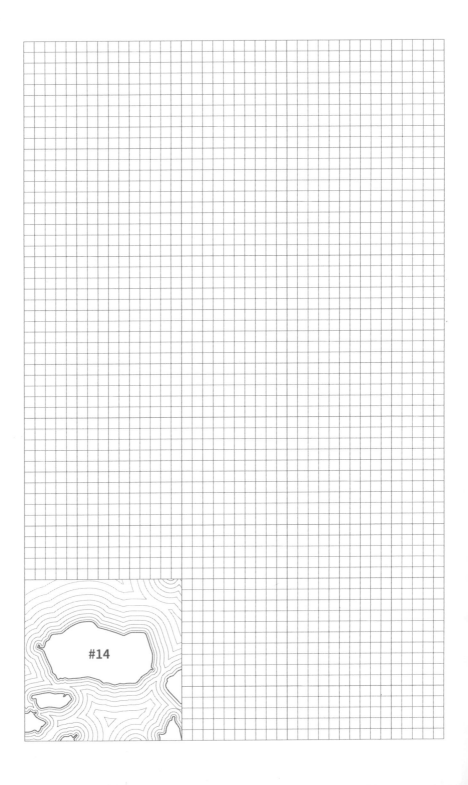

#14

MAP

18

A TOAST TO FOLLIES

The map: OS Explorer enlarged to 1:20 000 scale

The story: I'll have the 14-year-old malt please

If you approach Oban on one of the Hebridean island ferries you'll easily spot the unfinished folly of McCaig's Tower, a large arched ring on the top of Battery Hill. John Stuart McCaig commissioned the work in 1895, aged 72, with one of his aims being to support local masons with work during the winter months. As a result, construction proceeded slowly until his death in 1902. His bequest to continue the work was challenged by his relatives and the folly was left as we see it today. Within the circumference of the stone wall is a small park giving excellent views over Oban and the Isle of Mull beyond. Looking down towards the harbour you'll also spot the factory chimney of Oban distillery – one of the oldest in Scotland and the very last still in the heart of a town. The distillery was established by local brothers Hugh and John Stevenson in 1794 on the site of an older brewery, and became a major employer, influencing the growth of Oban. Constrained by the town that expanded around it, the distillery remains one of the smallest whisky makers in Scotland with just two stills.

▩ Easy

1. Can you find a building that has a cross-shaped hole in the middle of it?

2. How many caves are marked on the map? And how many places of worship?

▩ Medium

3. Which location sounds like a high point for preachers?

4. Can you find a location on the map that is an anagram of the phrase ROBOT HANGMAN?

▩ Tricky

5. Begin at the caravan site and head south along the road. At the first roundabout take the first exit, then on the next roundabout take the second exit. Follow the road until you can turn left onto another of the same class. Turn left at the church and follow the road until it degrades. What is the sum of the black spot heights your route has passed alongside?

6. Which former cable TV company, that ultimately was rebranded as Virgin Media, shares its name with a label on this map?

▩ Challenging

7. Find Cnoc Poll a'Mhinisteir and Cnoc Càrnach. Using the map information, what could you assume that 'cnoc' means?

8. Which Gaelic place names on the map do you think have the following English meanings?
   a. Michael's Rock
   b. Large Marsh
   c. Black Lake
   d. Large Ridge

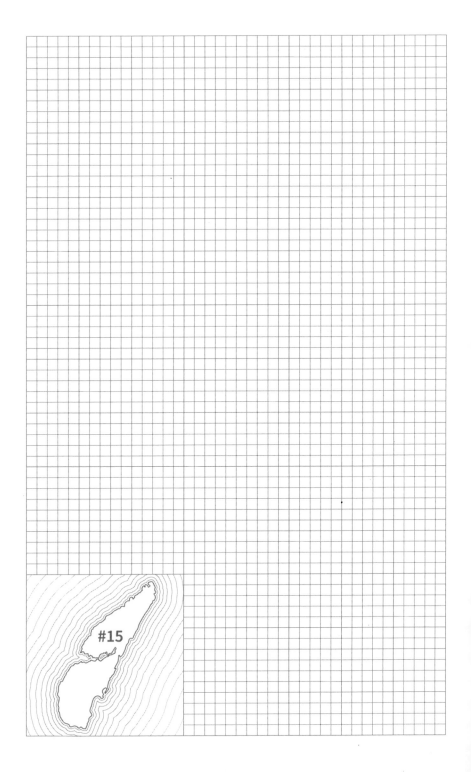

#15

MAP
19

BLOWN AWAY

The map: OS Landranger enlarged to 1:40 000 scale

The story: Ancient rocks from the ocean crust

Shetland is one of three geoparks in Scotland that celebrate the remarkable geology of Scotland; these rocks have shaped its history and the way of life across the archipelago. At the Keen of Hamar on Unst you can walk across rocks that were once part of an ancient ocean floor and experience a landscape that has changed little in the last 12,000 years. The metamorphic bedrock in this part of the island formed between 419 million and 1 billion years ago. Covered by thin soils, this geological reserve is home to some unique plants adapted to survive on these serpentine (mineral-rich) rocks. If you think it is a bit windy here on this headland you should head up to the top of the map and visit Saxa Vord with its tiny RAF radar station. You are now further north than St Petersburg in Russia and on the same latitude as Anchorage in Alaska. The Isles of Scilly, where we started, are over 1,200 km (780 miles) away. Saxa Vord is the highest point on Unst and holds the unofficial record for wind speed in Britain; in 1992 it reached 317 km/h (197 mph) before the measuring equipment blew away.

Easy

1. Can you find four masts stood close together? Why are they located there?

2. How many ancient sites, labelled with a Gothic font, can you find on the map?

Medium

3. Which is at a greater elevation: the building immediately east of the Ward of Norwick label, or the building due west of it by Sothers Field?

4. Which location sounds like a safe place for seafaring vessels?

Tricky

5. How far is the most easterly National Trust for Scotland property from the triangulation point?

6. Can you find what would be a namesake of a European island country, were its first letter to be different?

Challenging

7. Start at the most westerly cave and travel uphill in an easterly direction until you come to a small, enclosed body of water. There is a track next to this – follow the track south and take the second left, then the second right. Head south until you reach a T-junction. Follow the track north-east until you reach another T-junction, then turn right. Follow this road south, turning left then right, until you reach a place by a ruin. What is that ruin?

8. Start at a misspelt ancient Greek capital, and travel along the coast to a misspelt fast food. How many stacks have you passed along the way?

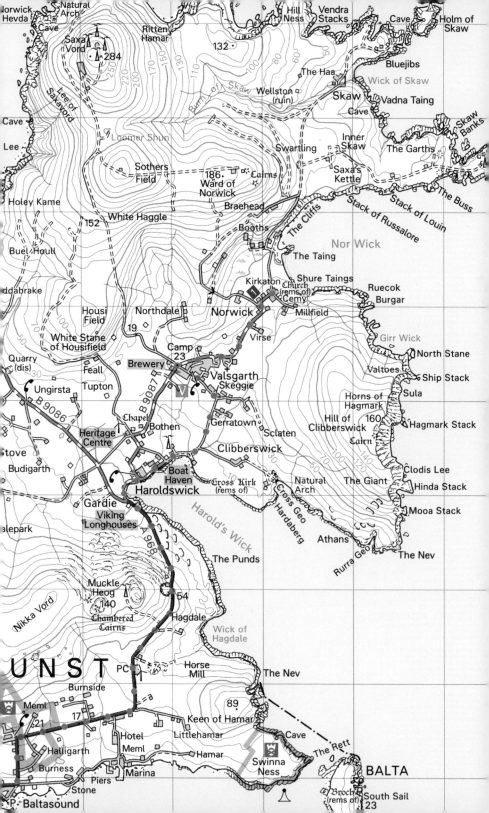

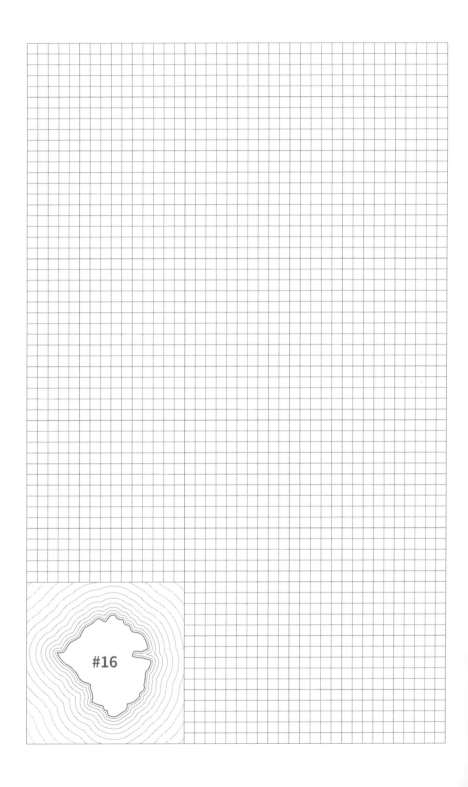

#16

MAP
20

DEFINITELY A PLACE WITH MORE COLOURS THAN BLACK

The map: OS Road enlarged to 1:210 000 scale

The story: The Black Isle

Now on the eastern side of Scotland, we finish our inadequately brief tour with a look at the Black Isle, which is not an island but a long, low peninsula separated from the surrounding mountains by the sea inlets of Cromarty and Moray Firth. Chanonry Point near Fortrose is one of the best places in Scotland, if not Europe, to try to spot bottlenose dolphins. The origin of its name is unknown, but the Black Isle's dark rich soils and its appearance from across the Firth are perhaps an indication. From the cliffs and hills above Fortrose it is sometimes possible to spot the highest mountain in Britain, Ben Nevis, at the other end of the Great Glen – although, as it's over 100 km (62 miles) away, you're probably better off looking for fossils along the shoreline. The pioneering amateur geologist Hugh Miller, born in Cromarty in 1802, studied the geology and fossil fish of the area and the title of his popular book *The Old Red Sandstone* is still used to collectively describe the sedimentary rocks deposited as a result of mountain-building activity (Caledonian orogeny) during the late Silurian and Devonian periods.

▨ Easy

1. How many walks or trails are marked on the map, further north than Moniack Castle?

2. Can you count how many map labels include the word 'Easter'?

▨ Medium

3. Can you find a place that shares its name with the Spanish word for chicken?

4. Where might you expect to find an eyrie, based purely on its name?

▨ Tricky

5. Starting at a historical battle site, travel almost due north until you reach a landmark currently in use guiding ships. Follow the coast to a viewpoint, and then travel due west to a place of temporary accommodation. What marks the viewpoint due north of here?

6. How much further is it along the road than it is as the crow flies, to travel from one service station to the other?

▨ Challenging

7. In what way are the man who watched a falling apple, and the man who wrote about a sinful apple, neighbours?

8. If it came back inside, where might you find Christmas?

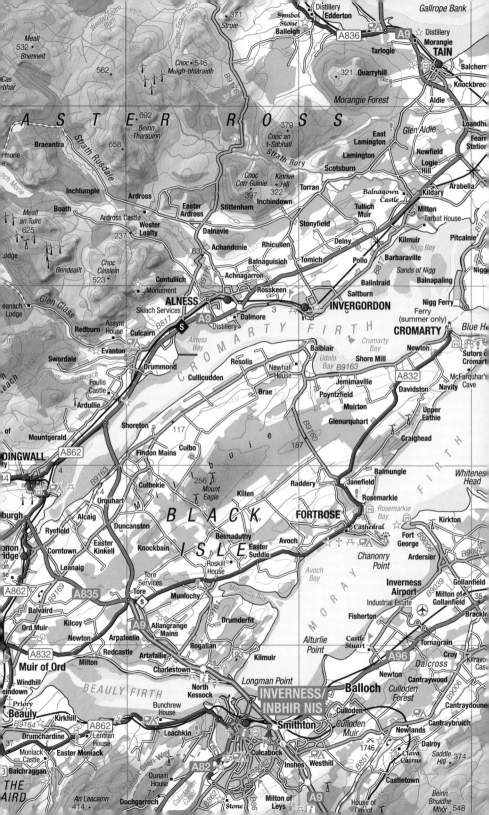

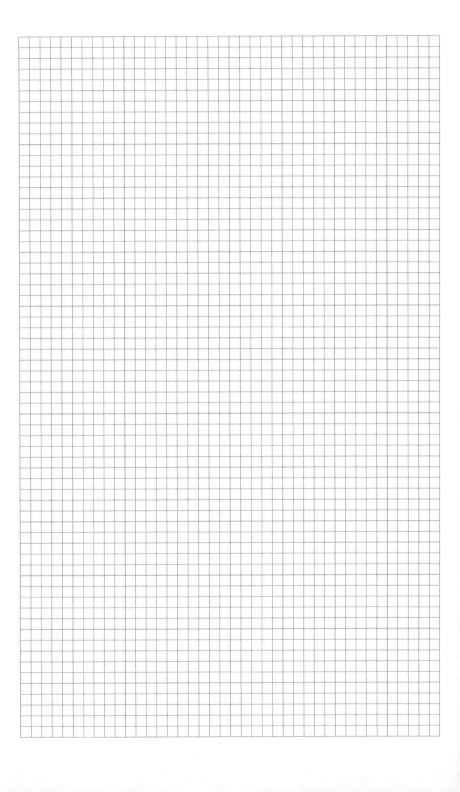

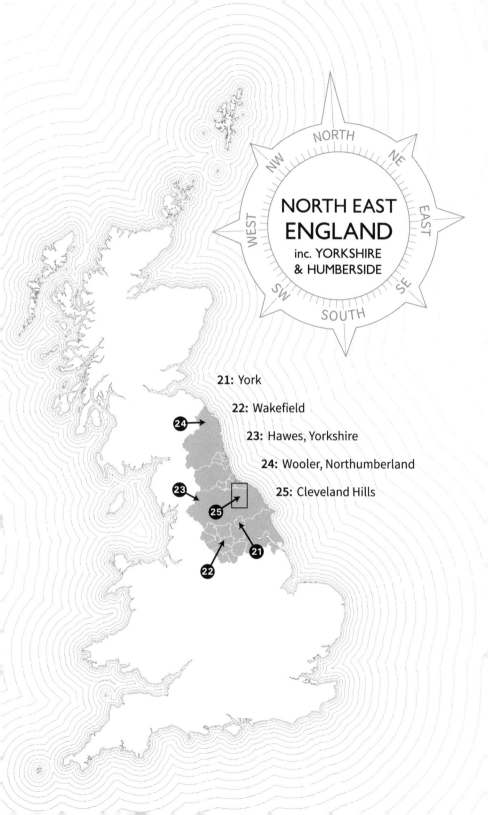

NORTH EAST
ENGLAND
inc. YORKSHIRE
& HUMBERSIDE

21: York

22: Wakefield

23: Hawes, Yorkshire

24: Wooler, Northumberland

25: Cleveland Hills

GET OUTSIDE!

Name: Dave Wilson

Who are you?
Long-distance walker and Northumberland trails and tour guide.

In three words, sum up what makes your area the best part of GB
Heritage. Landscape. People.

You favourite walk
My favourite walk is the 24 km (15 miles) of Hadrian's Wall that runs through Northumberland National Park. Starting near the remains of a third century Roman temple, it takes you along rugged crags, famous landmarks and a UNESCO World Heritage Site.

Your favourite view
My favourite panorama is from Whernside in the Yorkshire Dales National Park – it features scarred hillsides and valleys, dotted with signs of the area's industrial heritage such as the Ribblehead Viaduct.

Any local folklore?
The churchyard of St Cuthbert's in Bellingham has a stone inscribed with 'The Lang Pack', which is the final resting place of an unidentified man. One winter's night in 1723, a pedlar visited a local home to seek shelter. The servants refused but allowed him to leave his pack. That evening, a servant saw the pack move and shot it as a precaution, killing the man hiding inside. The servants realised the victim was planning to use a whistle to summon his accomplices to raid the house. They blew his whistle and killed four members of the gang, but the man in the pack's identity was never discovered.

The perfect day out
I love a well-planned coast or countryside walk, a halfway stop at a historic spot for lunch from my bag, and then finishing with a traditional pub for a locally brewed pint and bait (food).

Why people should visit
The North East is ideal for those looking for honest local charm, rugged landscapes, and some of Great Britain's last remaining truly wild places.

MAP
21

WHAT A PONG

The map: OS 25-inch 1907 (hand tinted)

The story: Town gas

Methods to heat coal to give off gas became known through the 17th and 18th centuries but practical use of coal gas didn't start until Scottish engineer William Murdoch lit his house in Cornwall in 1792. His employers, Boulton and Watt, made steam engines in Birmingham then developed small gas works to light factories. The German entrepreneur Frederick Winsor demonstrated the use of manufactured gas to light London streets and obtained a Royal Charter to build the world's first public gas works in 1813. Despite the poor quality of light given off naked flames, gas lighting quickly became popular and almost every large town in Britain soon had its own gas works. The York Gas Light Company formed in 1822 at Monk Bridge, with its rival, the York Union Gas Light Company, starting in 1837. They amalgamated in 1844 to form the York United Gas Light Company. Many small town gas works closed in the 1950s with the production of gas from oil, which could be piped at higher pressure over longer distances. The era of natural gas supplied directly through a distribution network completed the switch from coal gas in the 1960s.

◼ Easy

1. How many chimneys are labelled on this map? These are abbreviated to 'Chy'.

2. Which of the two named bridges is taller? And does the river flow northwards or southwards across the map area?

◼ Medium

3. What street's name suggests that it would be much faster to cycle in one direction than the other?

4. Can you find a stereotypical Englishman?

◼ Tricky

5. Starting at the benchmark on the road-facing side of the County Hospital, walk north-east to the end of the path, then follow the bank south to the first benchmark. What is its height?

6. Which location sounds like an ecclesiastical quarrel?

◼ Challenging

7. A lot meant to chap, L down to war, L to cross, and back to gardens. Match this path to one of the largest letters on the map.

8. How might you avert terminal damage?

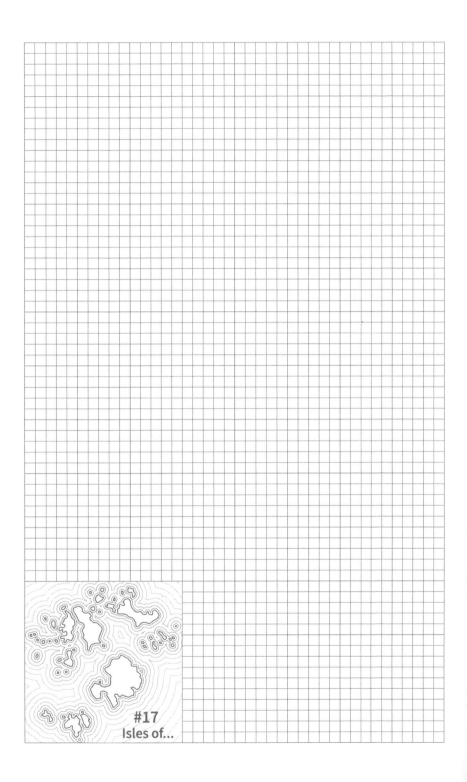

#17
Isles of...

MAP
22

RHUBARB BUT NO CUSTARD

The map: Open Map Local Vector at 1:8 000 scale

The story: Wakefield's unique triangle

The historic cathedral city of Wakefield, with its ancient market, rich trading history, industrial success and cultural heritage, isn't the story here! We're going to shine a light on forced rhubarb – although we shouldn't as this would stop its growth. The Rhubarb Triangle, famous for producing early grown or 'forced' rhubarb, used to fall between Leeds, Wakefield and Bradford but has reduced in area and is now contained by Wakefield, Morley and Rothwell. The rhubarb plant is a native of Siberia and thrives in Yorkshire's wet, cold winters. The method for forcing it was developed in the 1800s; the plants spend two years growing outside, storing carbohydrates in their roots, then, after a bit of frost, they are moved into warm, dark sheds which forces them to grow their sour-sweet stalks. In the late 19th century, demand for rhubarb in London saw the Great Northern Railway run special express trains daily during the growing season. Yorkshire Forced Rhubarb gained EU Protected Designation of Origin status (PDO) in 2010 and its importance to the area is such that Wakefield even boasts a sculpture of the plant in Holmfield Park.

QUESTIONS

Easy

1. How many streets on the map use an arrow to show their location?
2. How many roads are crossed by rails?

Medium

3. Head north from Lady Lane, crossing under a road and turning right. When reaching a junction that could take you to the road you crossed under, turn left. Turn right at the end of this road and continue past the cathedral, following this road around to the right. Enter the roundabout and take the dual carriageway exit, then bear right and turn right, heading westwards when joining a different dual carriageway. Pass the retail park and take the first exit at the roundabout. Go under the tracks, take the first exit again and then the first left. Which road are you on?

4. On what street might you expect to find a matador?

Tricky

5. Which road sounds like it wants you to go somewhere else?
6. If you drew lines to join the following roads in order, what letter would you create? Can you find a location on the map that uses this letter?
   a. Stubley Street
   b. Almshouse Lane
   c. Cotton Street
   d. Mark Street

Challenging

7. As the crow flies, how far is it from a place full of leaves and spines to the location where a narrow-brimmed hat and an aristocrat meet?

8. Which location on the map shares its name with a type of medieval rental, which typically included a long, narrow plot of land?

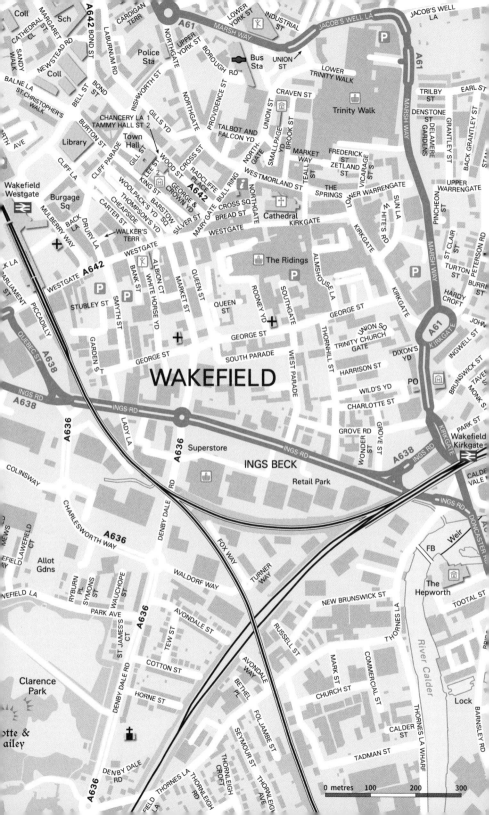

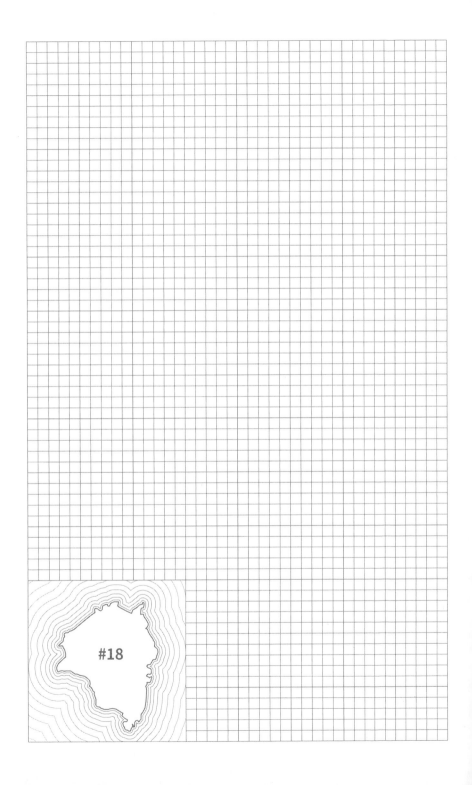

#18

MAP
23

NOW THAT'S WHAT
I CALL WATER MUSIC

The map: OS Explorer enlarged to 1:20 000 scale

The story: Hardraw Force

The waterfall at Hardraw has been a popular attraction since the 18th century, painted by Turner and described by Wordsworth in his guide to the Lakes: 'We walked up to the fall; and what would I not give if I could convey to you the feelings and images which where communicated to me?' It is no longer permitted to walk behind the fall as he described – 'the water fell at least ten yards from us and we stood directly behind it' – unless, of course, you're making a Robin Hood movie. At 30 metres (100 feet), Hardraw Force is the highest single drop waterfall in England above ground, although it briefly lost its status in December 2015 when Storm Desmond brought heavy rains to Malham Cove, also in Yorkshire, with its 70-metre (230-foot) drop. Hardraw itself was hit by a great flood in 1899 which damaged the lip of the fall as well as buildings in the village. The landowner, Lord Wharncliffe, had it repaired and secured with iron stakes. The bandstand, folly-like buildings, bridge and paths also date back to this time. The fall is in a natural amphitheatre that, unusually, can only be accessed through the bar of the Green Dragon pub. The amphitheatre has great acoustics and hosts an annual brass band competition. I guess you can't beat a Dales brass band in full flood.

◼ Easy

1. How many labels indicating a spring or springs are labelled with blue text on the map?

2. Where might you go to take part in an aerial sport?

◼ Medium

3. Starting from Hawes, which direction along the National Trail is likely to be more strenuous in terms of climbing in the parts of the trail covered by this map? Northwards or southwards?

4. Which location on the map shares its name with a carnivorous fish?

◼ Tricky

5. If you were to draw lines connecting the following place names in order, can you find a place on the map where both its words start with the letter you would have drawn?

   The spring by Burnt Acres Road > Appersett > Spillian Green > Ashes > Spillian Green > High Bands > Blackburn Farm

6. How many times in total do the words 'low' or 'high' appear on the map, including within other words?

◼ Challenging

7. To the nearest quarter of an hour, how long would it take you to walk along the riverside from the footbridge at Haylands Bridge to the point where Hardraw Beck joins, assuming you were walking at a constant 3 km/h?

8. Which words on the map are revealed by the following cryptic crossword clues?

   a. Tense antler's prickles
   b. Woman heard in storm

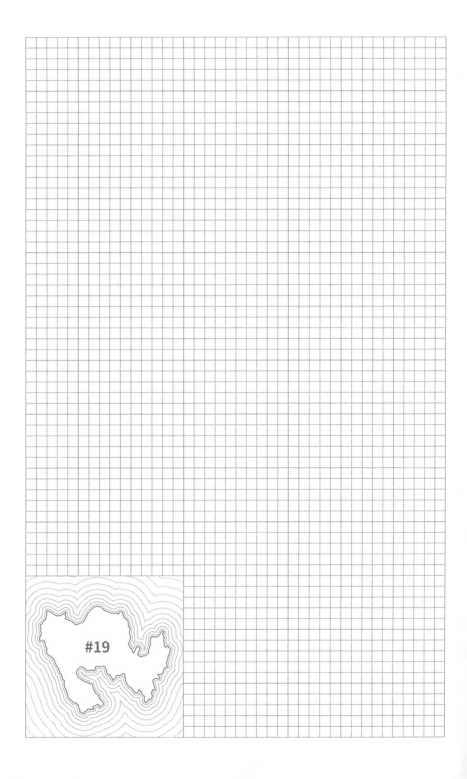

MAP 24

A LAWLESS WAY OF LIFE

The map: OS Landranger enlarged to 1:40 000 scale

The story: The Border reivers

From the 14th century through until the late 17th century, the lands that straddled the border between the sovereign nations of England and Scotland were very much a frontier lacking law and order, making it a buffer zone and difficult to cross. The area was remote and under-populated with its inhabitants more concerned with rivalries between clans and families than national allegiances. With the ever-present threat of war between the two countries, settled farming was impossible and raiding cattle (reiving) became an accepted way of life. Fortified houses and towers became common to protect families and their cattle. By the time of the reivers, Wooler was an established market town on one of the main routes north, east of the Cheviot Hills. Peel towers were built across the north of England to warn of attacks by both the Border reivers and the Scots. An act of the English Parliament in 1455 required each of the towers to have an iron basket on the top ready to make a smoke or fire signal. In the end it was during the more settled times that followed that Wooler was devastated by a series of fires of its own making; the worst was in 1863 which saw most of its historic centre destroyed.

Easy

1. Can you find the following spectacles-like marking on the map: 👓 ?
2. The date of a historic battle is marked on this map. In which year did it take place?

Medium

3. Starting at the top of a hill with a spot height of 326 metres, travel down the steepest edge of the hill and travel downstream to a road. Turn left and continue until you reach a public phone. What cheerful dale is now south of your position?
4. To the nearest kilometre, what is the distance as the crow flies between the two bridges over the Wooler Water that also contain on-road cycle routes?

Tricky

5. What is the mean height of all three triangulation pillars?
6. How many 'politicians' can you count on the map?

Challenging

7. Replace each word below with a synonym in order to find three locations on the map:
   a. Crowning timber
   b. Loom bird
   c. Guard mount

8. Starting on a map label that implies an area of honourable principle, descend by 10 metres onto a large plain, and head north-east to a crossing. Next, travel due west to an eastern place. Travel south as the crow flies until you reach a coniferous wood. Across a track, this wood will become non-coniferous. Follow the path of this woodland until you reach an ancient landmark. What is it?

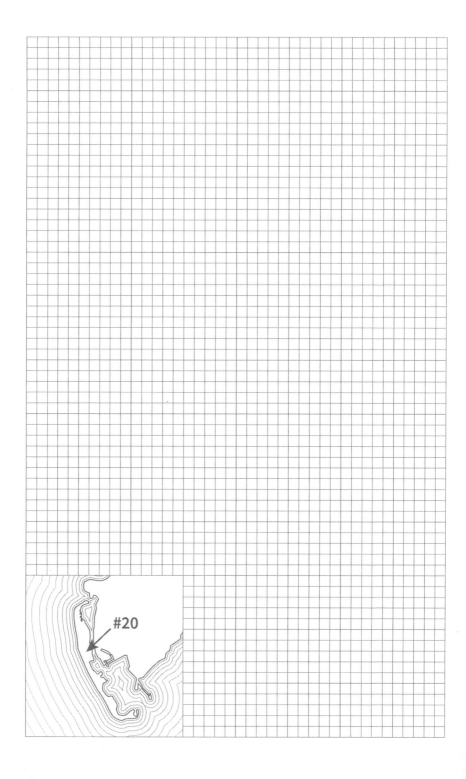

#20

MAP
25

SHAPED BY HISTORY

The map: OS Road enlarged to 1:210 000 scale

The story: Roseberry Topping

Middlesbrough became the first town in England to owe its existence to a railway. Joseph Pease was looking to develop a new shipping port for his coal and acquired land east of Stockton, extending the railway to the new port in 1830. Both Middlesbrough and the Stockton and Darlington Railway grew rapidly. However, by the end of the 1840s the pioneering railway had run into financial trouble and was almost taken over when ironstone was discovered on nearby Eston Beacon by John Marley of Bolckow in 1850. This rapidly transformed Middlesbrough with new blast furnaces and ironworks which the railway could serve with both coal and mineral iron, leading to extensive mining and quarrying in the Cleveland Hills which is still evident today. The distinctive outcrop of Roseberry Topping, which overlooks Middlesbrough and provides magnificent views across the Cleveland plain, was made by ironstone quarrying. Its cone shape was transformed in 1912 when a rock fall exposed one face of the mountain. Although blamed on the Roseberry ironstone mine workings under the summit, it was probably heavy rain that washed away the earth that acted as a support to the rock face. Now dubbed the Matterhorn of the Cleveland Hills, its shape has become an icon for the area.

Easy

1. How many public phones are marked on the map?
2. Imagine a straight line between the words Square Corner and Ampleforth, and another straight line joining Chop Gate and No Caravans. At what location do the lines cross?

Medium

3. Can you find a hillside chalk picture that can be seen from the A19?
4. Starting at the southernmost youth hostel (marked with an appropriate symbol), take the northern road and stop when you reach a public phone. Cross over a ridge to another public phone. Follow the nearby river south to where it is joined by another stream, then continue in a south-easterly direction. Stay on the river as it widens until it passes directly through the symbol for a building of historic interest. What is the name of the village directly west of this building?

Tricky

5. Can you find watercourses (or places named after watercourses) whose names match the following descriptions?
   a. sign of peace
   b. somewhere people often creep up on one another
   c. sharp-toothed valley

6. Starting at the highest point on the map, start travelling east along the footpath and continue following it until it becomes a road. Follow this to a junction, and turn right. Stay on this road, turning right as you cross over the last of three streams. Where is the nearest place to board?

Challenging

7. As the crow flies, how far is it from an 'everyday valley' to a 'lucky Scottish church'?
8. Can you find locations on the map that are anagrams of the following words or phrases? Ignore the spaces and punctuation, which may differ from those in the place names.
   a. NOT ANT
   b. YELL IT TO ANT
   c. GRAND RUG LID
   d. MAD GREEN ORATOR

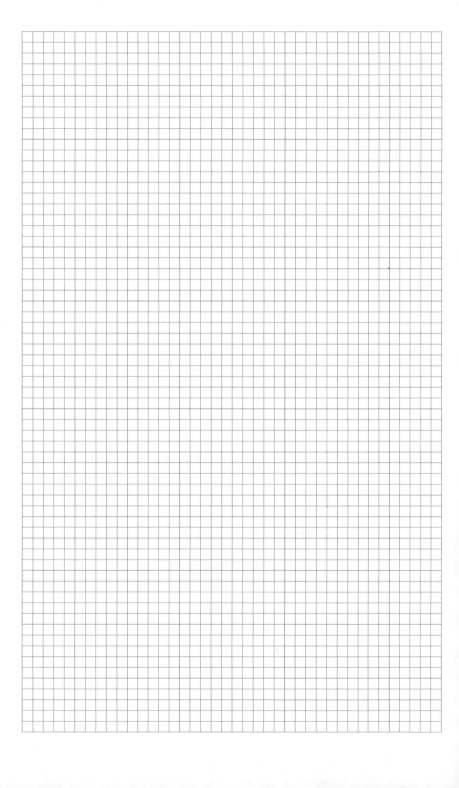

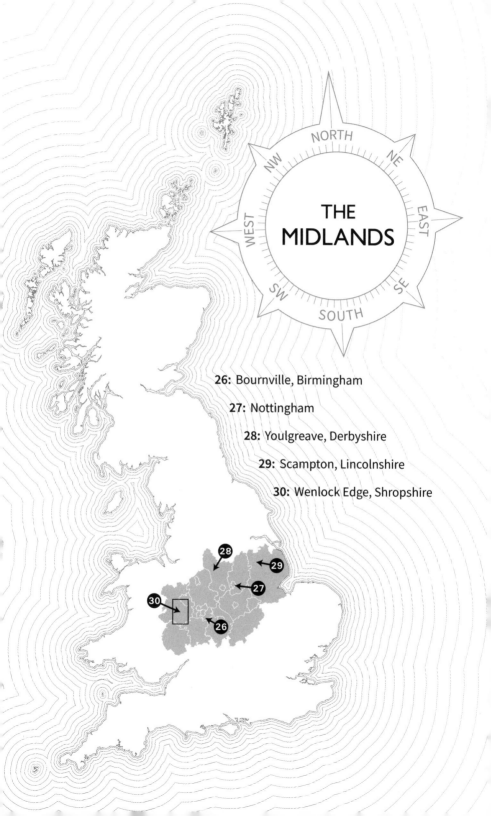

THE MIDLANDS

GET OUTSIDE!

Name: Get Out with the Kids

Who are you?

We are 'Get Out with the Kids', GetOutside Champions and a website dedicated to helping families get the most out of the outdoors.

In three words, sum up what makes your area the best part of GB

Close to everything.

Your favourite walk

Up and over our local Long Mynd hills in Shropshire.

Your favourite view

Looking at the hills and valley from Wentnor Church.

Any local folklore?

There is an outcrop of rock known as the Devil's Chair on the Stiperstones hill. Folklore says that when the clouds are covering the top of the hill, the Devil is in his chair.

The perfect day out

Walking, cycling or canoeing through the countryside, and stopping for a picnic or visiting one of the many historic pubs for a bite to eat.

Why people should visit

It's true that when most people think of the West Midlands, cities, towns, motorways and factories first come to mind. There is a lot of industrial heritage in the area, including the first iron bridge and first metal-framed building, which led to the modern skyscrapers. That industrial heritage left a network of canals to walk, cycle or canoe, and old railway lines that are now traffic-free cycle routes, with former train stations as welcoming cafés.

But it's not just industry; there's a wealth of countryside too. The River Severn travels through the Marches, an area full of old castles and medieval towns. There are plenty of hills, forests and moorland to discover, criss-crossed with footpaths and bridleways. So be it heritage or nature, the West Midlands has much to offer.

MAP
26

A SWEET PLACE TO LIVE AND WORK

The map: OS 25-inch 1903 (hand tinted)

The story: The factory in a garden

By the time George and Richard Cadbury took over their father's growing chocolate business in 1861, space for expansion was limited at their Bridge Street factory in central Birmingham. Like any business today, good communications were important and they were reliant on the canals for milk deliveries and the railways for cocoa imported through the ports of London and Southampton. Plans for a new branch of the Birmingham West Suburban Railway led them to a greenfield site south of Birmingham at Bournbrook Hall. The branch line served northern Worcestershire and at this point ran alongside the Worcester and Birmingham Canal. They named their new site after the local river Bourn and added ville (town) in a nod to their French rivals in the confectionery business. The brothers were Quakers and aimed to look after their workers with improved working conditions and decent pay in a modern factory. They pioneered pension schemes and medical care and in 1893 George Cadbury bought, out of his own pocket, 120 acres of land next to the factory to create a model village with open spaces to 'alleviate the evils of modern, more cramped living conditions'. His ideas influenced garden cities in the 20th century and continue to resonate today.

◻ Easy

1. Can you find a road that sounds sharp to the touch?

2. Where on the map sounds like an appropriate place to pitch a tent?

◻ Medium

3. Can you find all three 'green' Monopoly street names on this map?

4. There are two streets on the map named after yellow-flowering trees. What are they?

◼ Tricky

5. Starting at 524, travel in a straight line to an island. From this island, travel directly east until you meet a named street. At this point, travel in a line that is parallel to the first line you followed, and stop this line when it reaches the same latitude as your starting point. What building have you arrived at?

6. What printed word on the map is the only one surrounded (entirely on the map) on all sides by train tracks?

◼ Challenging

7. Which location on the map shares its name with a football club's former home ground?

8. Which places on the map are being described here?
   a. Water carrier with panache
   b. Driver moulted
   c. Fodder is functional

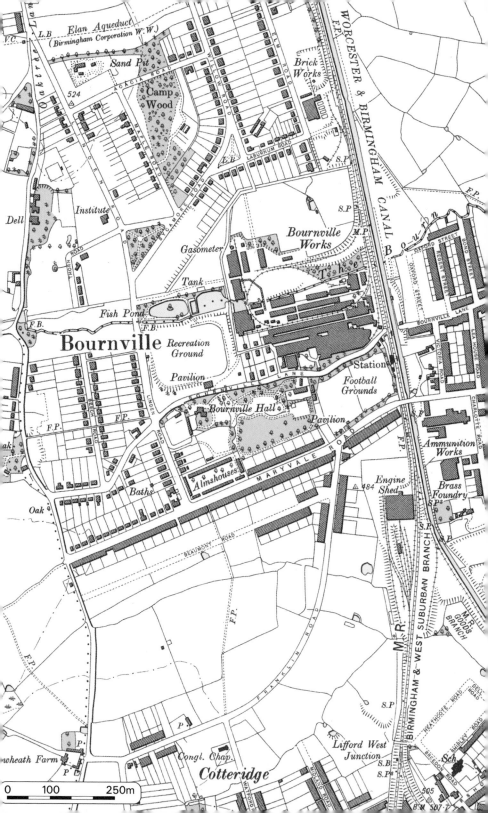

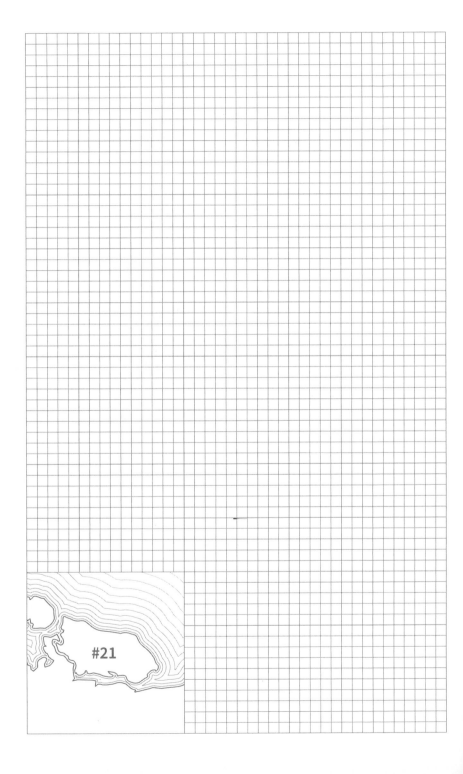

#21

MAP
27

RETURN OF THE TRAM

The map: Open Map Local Vector at 1:8 000 scale

The story: Keeping Nottingham moving

Like blood circulating around a body, a large city needs to keep everybody moving, getting people in and out without too many delays, and improving their health by reducing polluting traffic jams. Many large towns and cities across Britain developed extensive tram systems in the late 19th century; first with horse- and steam-powered trams, then electric. Most had disappeared by the mid-20th century in favour of the more flexible motor bus and the demand for road space from private cars. With cars clogging up the city centre and overcrowded buses, cities like Nottingham have been reintroducing trams. Nottingham's system is 32 km (20 miles) in length and runs from the suburbs into the city centre, linking with the park and ride sites and Nottingham railway station. Expansion of the system has been considered to provide airport and motorway links as well as the proposed high-speed railway, HS2. Reducing congestion, pollution and carbon emissions will drive cities to find solutions that keep their centres vibrant and attractive places.

▦ Easy

1. Can you find a word on the map that contains the letter 'Z'?
2. Can you find the surnames of two US presidents on the map?

▦ Medium

3. If you drew a line joining the blue shopping centre symbols, and a second line joining the westernmost and easternmost parking symbols, then on what street would these lines intersect?
4. Find all three places of worship with a spire, minaret or dome and connect them to form a triangle. Can you find, within this triangle, a street whose first word can be found elsewhere on the map?

▦ Tricky

5. Starting at Nottingham Station, take a tram northbound and alight at the third stop. Head north-west, and turn right at the first junction. Take the first left, and turn right onto the bard's street. then turn right at the end of the road and go straight over the crossroads. Take the second left, then go straight until you can turn onto a street that sounds bumpy. At the end of this road, turn onto an empty version of this road. Where are you?
6. Can you find an angry 24-hour period?

▦ Challenging

7. Begin on the most westerly of two roads whose name is a synonym for 'dogs'. Exit the road and turn left. At the end of the road, travel away from the castle. Add three to the value of your current street, turning left at the tram line. Stay on this road through two street changes, then turn right opposite a 'container' street. When facing a sheep product, turn right. Turn into a road which links back to where you began. Where are you?
8. Starting at the 'garden of England', fly north-west over two men to a road that could be Scottish or Antipodean. Which London tube station shares its name with an adjacent road?

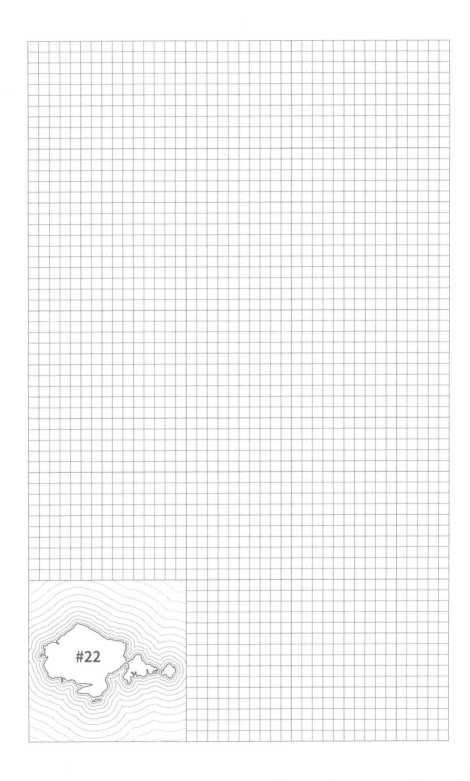

#22

MAP
28

THAT'S A WELL-DRESSED WELL

The map: OS Explorer enlarged to 1:20 000 scale

The story: Youlgreave's waterworks

Before the development of distributed water supplies, domestic water was either drawn directly out of wells or taken from nearby springs and rivers. In places like Youlgreave in the Peak District, low river levels in the summer would lead to an increase in sickness and death, particularly amongst children. During the 19th century, villages and towns built waterworks to improve their water supply. Funds for repairs and improvements had to be raised by the villagers and in time these local waterworks were superseded by larger, more efficient water companies and then regional waterboards, which have since been privatised. In Youlgreave, spring water was piped to a cistern with a capacity of 6,800 litres (1,500 gallons), which would fill up overnight and be unlocked in the morning by a waterkeeper. Uniquely, Youlgreave has retained its own non-profit water company for its 500 households. It improved the supply in the village in 1869 by piping in another spring and increasing the number of taps to ten along the main street. The cost of the works was paid in kind by the able-bodied men of the village contributing three days' labour. To celebrate, the village revived the custom of dressing wells with flowers. Today, well-dressing is a popular event held all over Derbyshire during the spring and summer months, although in Youlgreave it could almost be called tap-dressing.

QUESTIONS

▨ Easy

1. How many historic sites are marked on the map? They are indicated by a Gothic font.

2. Which farm shares its name with a famous US building?

▨ Medium

3. What place on the map sounds like it might grow even more maps?

4. Start on the northernmost footbridge on the River Lathkill, then follow the river in a south-easterly direction until you reach the second road crossing. Exit on the side with the steepest incline, and follow the bridleway north until you reach a point used for triangulation. Join the road and continue in the same direction until you meet the civil parish boundary. Continue to follow it off the road eastbound until you reach a small patch of woodland. What is the name of this place?

▨ Tricky

5. Which road shares its name with a small songbird, when one letter is changed?

6. As the crow flies, how far is it in kilometres from a shaded area that shares its name with a European sea to a rock face where you would be likely to find a narrow channel?

▨ Challenging

7. Each of the following routes traces out a letter. What are the letters, and which local almond-flavoured treat are they the initials of?
   • Burton Moor Farm > Coldwell End > Raper Mine > Meadow Place Grange > Noton Barn Farm > Burton Moor Farm
   • Hotel > Bradford > Alport > Bradford > the point where Bleakley Dike crosses the National Trail

8. If you split some words on the map into two words, then interpret each of them as having the meaning of those two words, which words on the map are being described by the following?
   a. Possessed senior academic
   b. Deer mound
   c. Leap chime

What do all these words have in common?

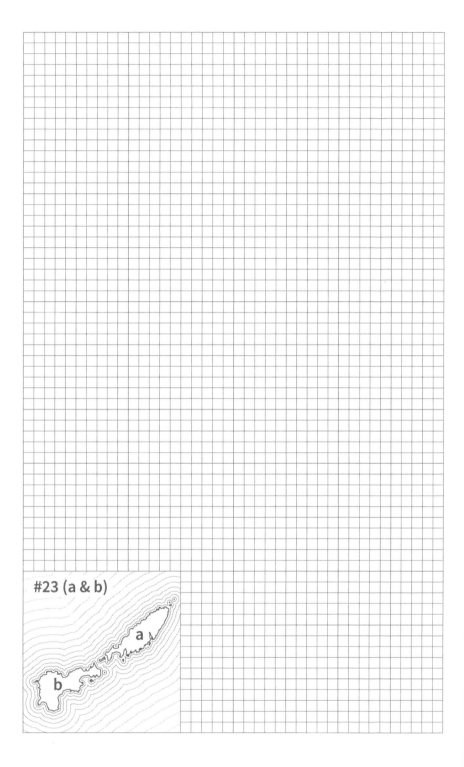

#23 (a & b)

a

b

MAP 29

THE A15 ARCHER

The map: OS Landranger enlarged to 1:40 000 scale

The story: Vulcan bombers and the Cold War

As 'almost straight roads' go, you can't beat the A15 between Lincoln and Scunthorpe, which follows the Roman Road of Ermine Street for nearly all of its route to the River Humber. Unfortunately, this seemingly endless road was given a major kink across the fields of Lincolnshire in the 1950s to accommodate the runway extension required for the heavy Vulcan bombers which were part of Britain's nuclear deterrent during the Cold War. To the west of the airfield the land drops away as part of the Lincolnshire Edge, making an extension of the original runway in that direction impossible. The airfield first came into use in 1916 to counter the Zeppelin airships, but in 1919 its temporary hangers were removed and the site was returned to farmland. Expansion of the Royal Air Force in the 1930s saw the site reopened as RAF Scampton, a fully equipped bomber station that was home to the 617 Squadron, remembered today as the 'Dam Busters'. With aircraft weights increasing, the station was closed between August 1943 and October 1944 for new concrete runways and buildings. In 1955, Scampton became one of ten RAF stations to operate the new long-range Vulcan jet bombers. The diverted A15 was incorporated into the longbow of the station badge with the arrow angled like the runway. Currently a training base and home to the Red Arrows display team, RAF Scampton is expected to close by 2022.

▨ Easy

1. How many pools or reservoirs are on the map, counting only those further north than the most southerly phone box? Don't count moats or the spring.

2. Can you find a central-sounding road?

▨ Medium

3. From the point where two Romans meet, if you follow the stoat's coat to the map edge will you ascend or descend?

4. Starting at the triangulation pillar, drive to a viewpoint. Turn right and continue straight until the road reaches an elevation of 50 metres. Head due north to a precipice. Where are you?

▨ Tricky

5. How far is it, as the crow flies, from the most northerly water defence to the body of water surrounded by embankments on three sides?

6. Add together the road numbers that appear on the map, and add together all of the black spot heights that are adjacent to the B road. Do not repeat any number, even if it appears more than once on the map. Which digit from the answer to the second calculation does not appear in the first?

▨ Challenging

7. Imagine a triangle formed between the three locations: four nearby places of worship; a hall that lies on the opposite edge of the map to its name; and a farm that is also a home. Combining two words within this shape, which famous literary character's name can you form?

8. Can you find locations on the map that are anagrams of the following words or phrases? Ignore the spaces and punctuation, which may differ from those in the place names.
   a. LEO, WILL
   b. NOT CAMPS
   c. ART BY BELT
   d. CONTOURS HALT
   e. COIN BORN BLUNTLY

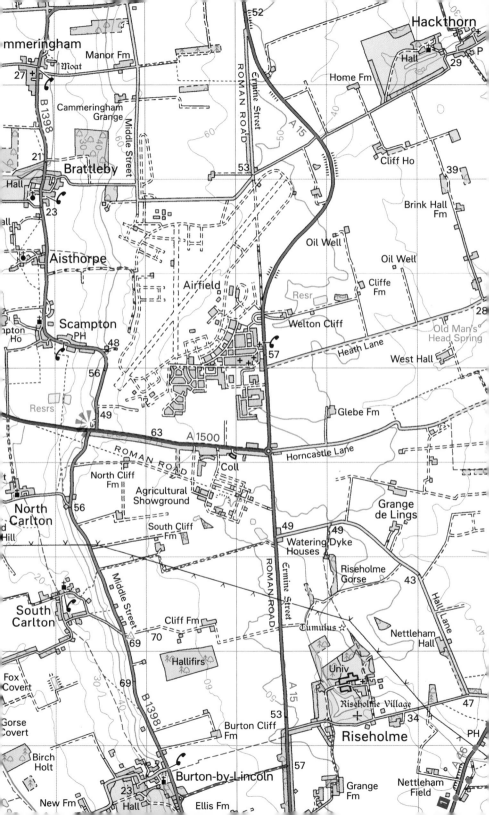

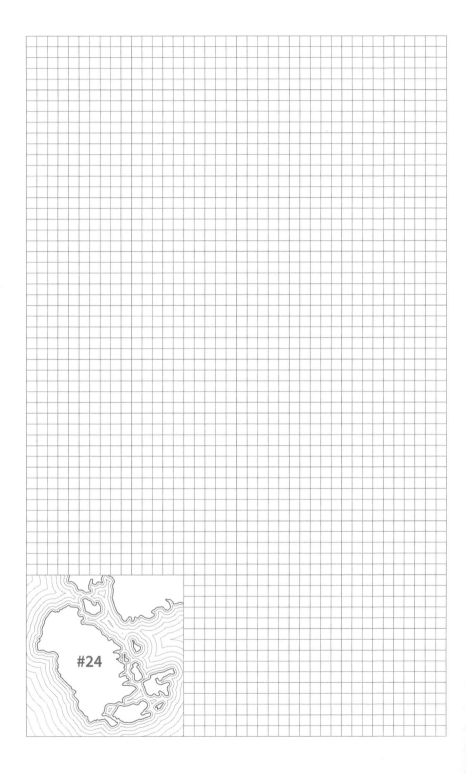

#24

MAP
30

LIME AWAY

The map: OS Road enlarged to 1:210 000 scale

The story: Wenlock Edge

Wenlock Edge runs unbroken for nearly 30 km (18 miles) from Craven Arms to Ironbridge and is one of the best examples of a limestone escarpment in Britain. Its steep wooded hills support a wide diversity of plant life including rare orchids and provide great views across the Shropshire countryside. The narrow ridge of limestone was laid down over 400 million years ago when Shropshire was a warm, shallow sea just below the equator, and its ancient corals and seashells can be found today as fossils. This organic sedimentary rock has been used since Roman times to make lime for plaster, mortar and concrete. The process was often carried out close to where it was needed and the kilns then dismantled and moved to a new site or left to decay. Remains of pot kilns can be found near Much Wenlock. As Britain industrialised in the 18th century, new uses for lime increased demand and kilns that could run continuously were developed. Limestone quarries also had to supply the new iron foundries, where lime was added to the iron ore in the blast furnaces to remove impurities. The new Cross Britain Way recreational path runs along the ridge to the River Severn, past old quarries and the historic Iron Bridge.

▨ Easy

1. How many viewpoints are marked on the map?

2. How many times does the word 'brook' appear on the map, either on its own or within another word?

▨ Medium

3. Find the place on the map that shares its name with a town in Oxfordshire that hosts a world-famous royal regatta. The maiden name of which royal bride can be found nearby?

4. Where is the highest point, and what is located there?

▨ Tricky

5. Start at the author of the Iliad, and join a nearby A road. Drive along it until you pass two optimistic place names on your right. Take the next left, and cross the staggered junction. What convenience have you arrived at?

6. How many solar farms are marked on the map?

▨ Challenging

7. Travel from the pop star known by a single name to the nearest rook, then head due east to find clues. Head ENE to alter ego Lily (paired with a palindrome), and then due north to the wartime ditch. Head WSW to singer Tony, and then to the nearest station. Travel one stop west. Where are you?

8. If you split some words on the map into two words, then interpret each of them as having the meaning of those two words, which words on the map are being described by the following?
   a. Equine fodder
   b. Construction used to be
   c. Crazier dream
   d. Fastener weight

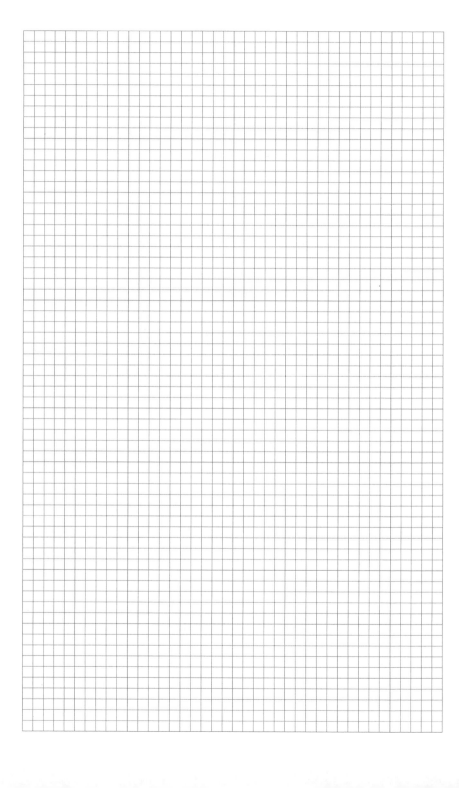

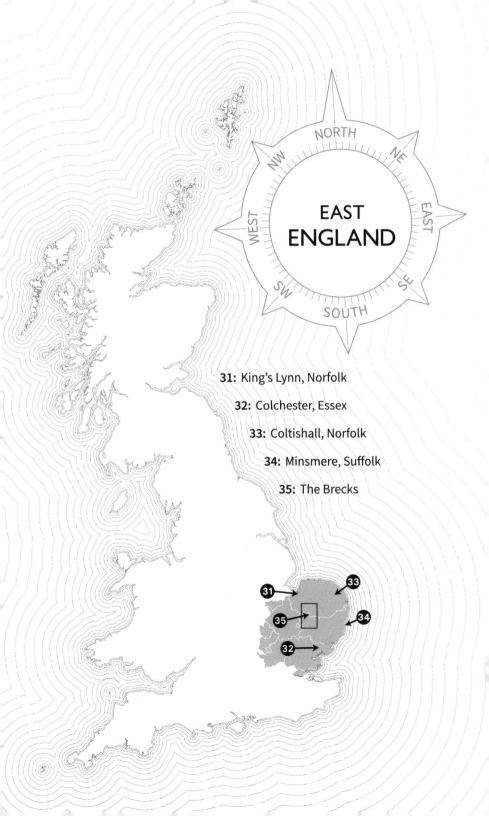

EAST
ENGLAND

NORTH
NW   NE
WEST   EAST
SW   SE
SOUTH

31: King's Lynn, Norfolk

32: Colchester, Essex

33: Coltishall, Norfolk

34: Minsmere, Suffolk

35: The Brecks

GET OUTSIDE!

Name: Alan Parkinson

Who are you?
I'm a teacher and geographer and have lived in East Anglia for over half my life.

In three words, sum up what makes your area the best part of GB
Subtle, coastal, independent.

Your favourite walk
A circular route through the pine woods backing the beach huts at Wells-next-the-Sea to the Victoria pub on the Holkham Estate, then back along the wide expanse of Holkham Beach with its dunes and salt marsh, often featured in lists of the best beaches in the world.

Your favourite view
The town of Southwold from the pier, with the lighthouse and beach huts behind the beach, and Victorian villas looking out to sea.

Any local folklore?
One of the most enduring East Anglian legends describes the devil dog: Black Shuck, an omen of death. Also, Kevin Crossley-Holland, one of the greatest living folklorists, lives and works in the region, reworking myths for modern readers.

The perfect day out
Assuming we could move quicker than the roads of the region permit, I'd have breakfast in Southwold, a stroll on Cromer Pier, crab salad and a pint of Wherry ale for lunch, a gentle walk through Wicken Fen, and finish with fish and chips on the beach in Hunstanton, an east coast resort where you can watch the sun set over the sea (work that out).

Why people should visit
This is a region that you have to make an effort to visit because it's not 'on the way' to anywhere else. 'Slow you down', as they say locally, and enjoy distant glimpses of the sea, quiet rural villages and wide vistas full of sky.

MAP
31

IN A LEAGUE OF ITS OWN

The map: OS 25-inch 1905 (hand tinted)

The story: The international port of King's Lynn

Set inland below the shallow waters of The Wash, King's Lynn doesn't readily spring to mind as an international port. These days it handles bulk goods less suited to the shipping container: metals, chemicals, agricultural and forest products. The biggest changes came with the incorporation of the King's Lynn Docks and Railway Company Act in 1865. This helped finance the building of the Alexandra Dock, although little of the rail network remains today. Back in the 13th century, King's Lynn was one of England's most important ports and was part of the Hanseatic League, trading in wool, cloth and salt. The League was a confederation of merchant guilds and market towns around the coasts of north-western and central Europe, established to protect their economic interests and trading routes. Beginning with a handful of north German towns in the late 12th century, the League grew until the mid-1400s. Then economic, political and social changes around the Baltic Sea and Europe led to the League diminishing until its final collapse in 1862.

◼ Easy

1. How many landing stages/stages are labelled?

2. How many times are mooring posts labelled on the map? Count each 'Mooring Posts', 'M.P' or 'M.Ps' once to reach your total.

◼ Medium

3. What appropriately named street abuts where fire engines are stored?

4. Where might Father Christmas live?

◼ Tricky

5. Start at a road that shares its name with a home county. Travel west, turning right at the triangulation pillar. Head north until you are by the entrance to a road where you might go to sell your wares. Which building is directly opposite you across the 'place'?

6. Can you find locations on the map that are anagrams of the following words or phrases? Ignore the spaces and punctuation, which may differ from those in the place names.

   a. BIGGER WINDS   c. TANS FRONTS

   b. STANDING GALE

◼ Challenging

7. Begin at a building that shares its first name with a Shakespearean theatre. Cross to a pub. Head between the buildings in a north-westerly direction until you reach railway tracks. Follow the tracks to the second of a pair of perpendicular crossroads. Turn right and follow the railway line to a benchmarked location. Find the benchmark that is exactly one less than this. Which building, that has not been referred to in either the subject or answer of another question on this page, is a short distance south of here?

8. If you split single words on the map into words or abbreviations, interpreted in the given order, which map words are being represented here?

   a. Sandwich street   c. Network chime

   b. Label alien   d. Low peal

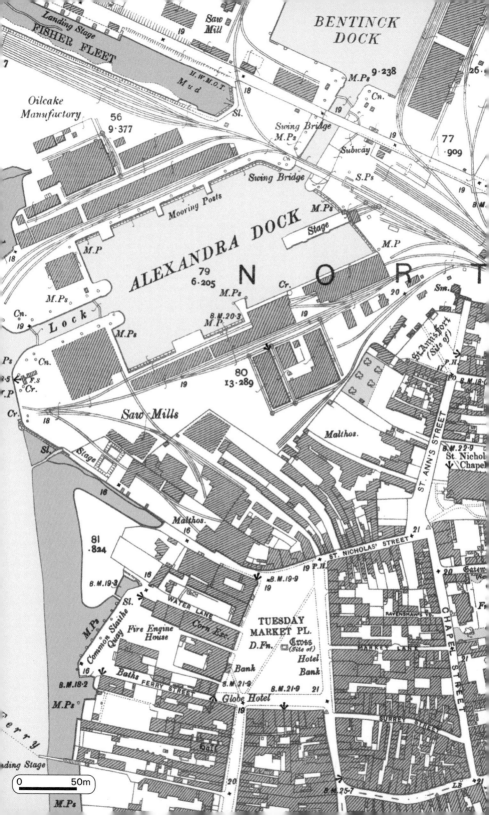

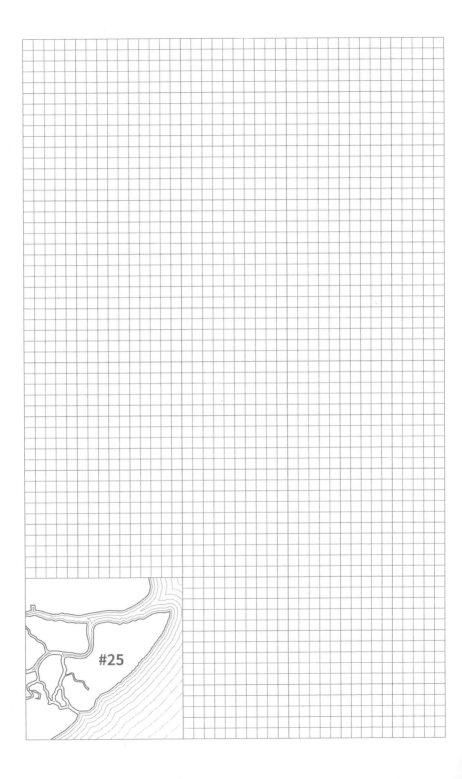

#25

MAP
32

ALL ROADS LEAD TO . . .

The map: Open Map Local Vector at 1:8 000 scale

The story: Assured retirement – Roman style

Britain in the late Iron Age was on the edge of the Roman Empire and traded with the Romans until the 40s AD, when the balance of power between the tribal kingdoms saw the Catuvellauni seize Camulodunum (Colchester), the capital of the Trinovantes. The first Roman campaign in 43 AD swept up through Kent (Cantiaci tribe) and into Essex using military force – which included elephants – to crush any British resistance. Camulodunum was the first capital of Roman Britain and the first place in Britain to be given the status of a Roman Colonia, a planned settlement for veteran soldiers who became Roman citizens upon discharge. This symbol of Roman control and lifestyle became the target of a British uprising, led by Queen Boudicca of the Iceni tribe, which resulted in the town being sacked and burned in 60 AD. After this, Londinium (London) became the capital as the Romans pushed west and north, settling Britannia under Roman government for nearly 400 years.

◼ Easy

1. How many places of worship with a tower, spire, minaret or dome are marked on the map?

2. Which street sound like a great way to get somewhere faster?

◼ Medium

3. The ancient Roman name for Colchester, Camulodunum, appears on the map as CAMVLODVNVM. Can you find another ancient Roman city on the map?

4. What sounds like the chief barrier to entry?

◼ Tricky

5. Can you find a 'snake-like' street?

6. Which street sounds like a way to rouse a meadow?

◼ Challenging

7. Where might Newton perambulate?

8. Imagine drawing lines as instructed below:

   - Draw a line from a place where an ancient resident might practise his tightrope skills, through the symbol for the second most southerly car park, until you reach the old city wall.
   - Draw a line from here to a road which is one rank less senior than a sergeant.
   - Now draw a line to a verdant educational establishment.
   - Draw a line back to where you began.

   Which municipal facility are you highlighting?

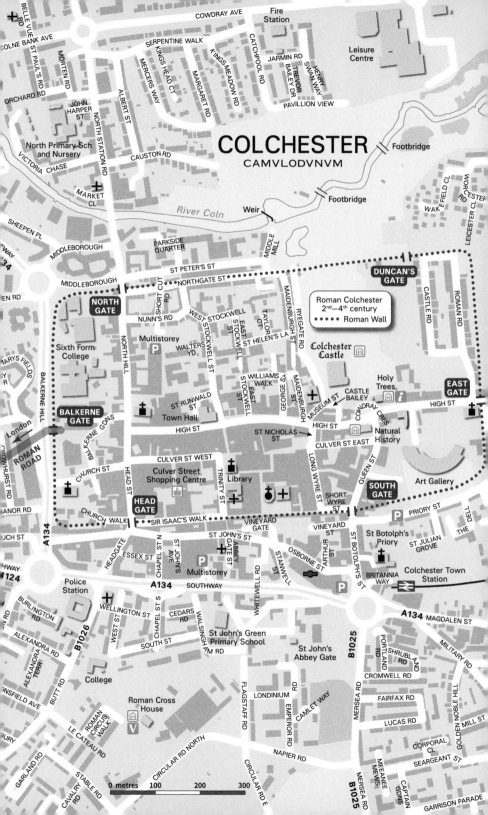

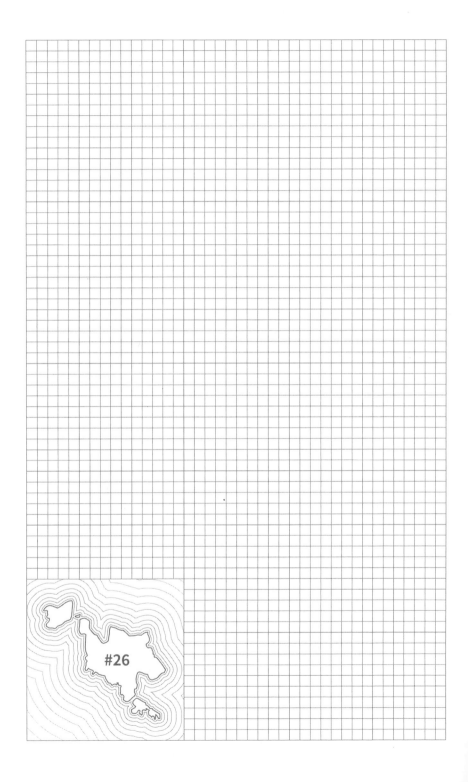

#26

MAP
33

MALTINGS AND WHERRIES

The map: OS Explorer enlarged to 1:20 000 scale

The story: Coltishall connections

The river Bure continues to play an important part in the success of Coltishall in Norfolk. Before good-quality roads, water was the easiest means to trade with more distant settlements and, until about 1912, it was possible to navigate as far inland as Aylsham. Today the limit of navigation for powered craft is in Coltishall, just below the bridge for the B1150. The village also benefited from being on the 'high road', halfway between Norwich and North Walsham. When the railway arrived in 1879 it could only prosper from its connections across the county and further afield. The village became renowned as a centre for malting – turning barley into malt for the brewing industry. Sailing barges called wherries brought the barley to more than a dozen malthouses, with the processed malt leaving by railway or wherry to breweries as far away as London. Coltishall is reputed to be the birthplace of the wherry and it specialised in craft built for the narrower rivers of the Bure and Ant.

■ Easy

1. Can you find three historic sites? These are labelled using a Gothic font.
2. What is the highest elevation shown on the map?

■ Medium

3. Imagine connecting the three public telephones to form a triangle. What is the total of the contour and spot height numbers contained either within or overlapping the perimeter of this shape?
4. Can you find a place that might describe an incision made during surgery?

■ Tricky

5. If a hill town had establishments for depositing and saving money, they could be described as which map location?
6. From the labelled reservoir, head north along the B road, cross the river, and bear left at the junction to stay on the same road. Cross the railway line, then bear left onto a minor road and continue north. When this road passes a footpath on your right, follow that path to a small patch of woodland. What map label adjoins the woodland?

■ Challenging

7. If you drew a straight line from the middle of a heavenly spot to the centre of a place that sounds like it could be on the very edge of any map, then further extended this line onwards, what tourist and leisure symbol would it end on?
8. Begin at the spot height south of three fluid quadrilaterals. Cross south-eastwards to a diminished country of twenty-six cantons. Join the road at its end here, then follow it to a bridleway, and then follow that bridleway north until it reaches a road. Follow the road north, and turn shortly onto another bridleway. Continue along this path until it splits in two. How far is it, as the crow flies, to this end point from where you started?

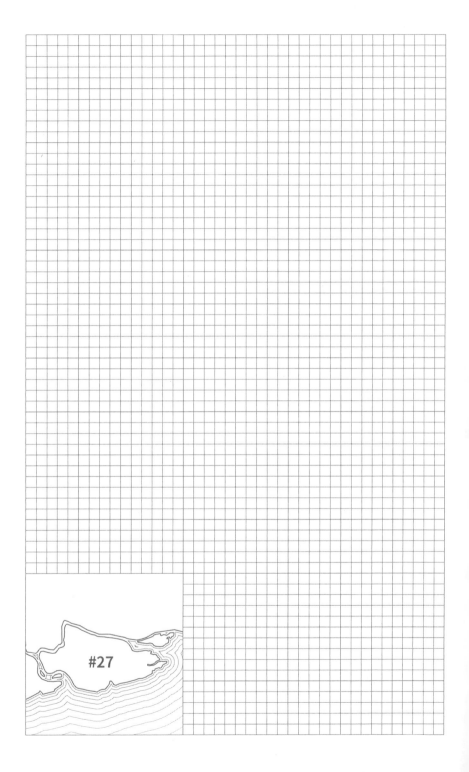

#27

MAP
34

WILDLIFE FROM WARFARE

The map: OS Landranger enlarged to 1:40 000 scale

The story: Minsmere Nature Reserve

By the early 20th century, the 'unproductive and unprofitable' marshes in Suffolk, like many across Britain, had been drained for agriculture. Fortunately for birdwatchers today, the threat of invasion at the start of the Second World War led to the reclaimed land behind the dunes at Minsmere being re-flooded as a quick solution to defending the low-lying coastline. The remains of concrete anti-tank cubes can still be found on the coastal dunes and a pillbox is hidden inside the ruin of the medieval chapel. The coastline here has always been under attack with the small village of Minsmere lost to coastal erosion by the 16th century. During the 18th century, this stretch of coast became a favourite haunt for smugglers and a coastguard station operated at Minsmere in the 1840s to try to control the untaxed contraband. After the Second World War, the flooded land was left as a wetland and since 1947 it has been managed as a reserve by the RSPB – encouraging a more welcome invasion of migrating birds.

■ Easy

1. Can you find two of each of the following?
   a. Cemeteries (abbreviated to 'Cemy')
   b. Museums (abbreviated to 'Mus')
   c. Masts

2. There are two (non-religious) towers marked on the map. Can you find them both?

■ Medium

3. Can you locate what sounds like a pile of cleaning tools?

4. Which pair of locations are further apart, as the crow flies: the two triangulation pillars; or the most westerly pub and the most easterly forestry commission site?

■ Tricky

5. Which place on the map shares its name with an observation module on the International Space Station?

6. What is the sum of the black spot heights, ignoring any duplicate values?

■ Challenging

7. Start on the road nearest the glasshouse, head east until you are by the first level crossing, then turn left. Head north on the same road until you reach a junction by a church with a tower. Turn right, go to the end of that road, then turn left. Follow this road to a junction, then head north-east and continue on this road until the National Trail breaks away from the on-road cycle route. Follow the National Trail until a junction with a footpath, and turn right. Follow the track until you reach a set of buildings. What are they?

8. Which locations on the map are represented by the following phrases? Each word in the original map locations has been replaced by a word that describes the original word.
   a. Tree club
   b. Season undercover
   c. Power-station constraints

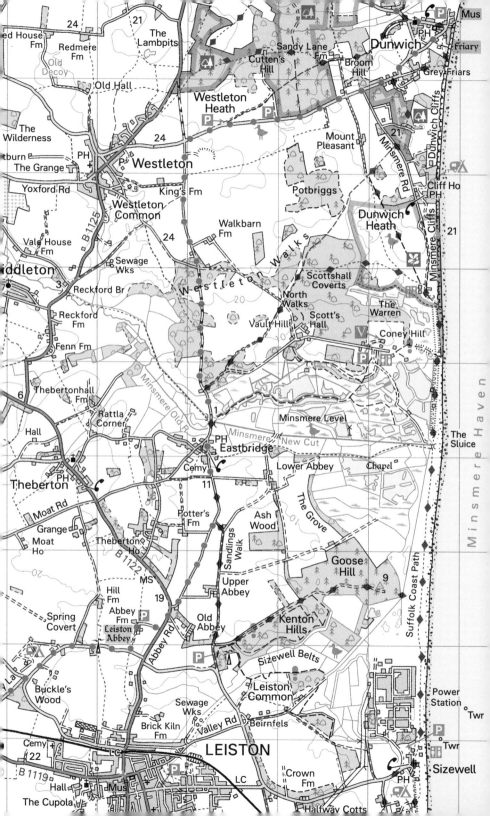

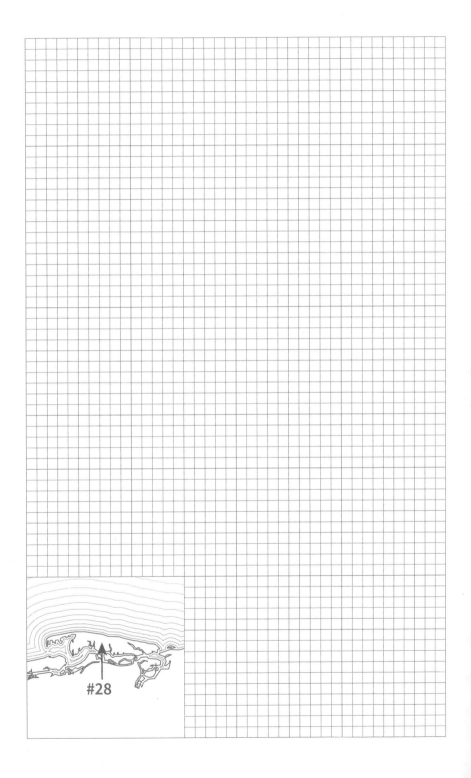

#28

MAP
35

NOT RABBIT STEW AGAIN!

The map: OS Road enlarged to 1:210 000 scale

The story: The Brecks

In the heart of East England is one of the great natural areas of Britain. The Brecks covers over 1,000 km² (almost 400 square miles) of once-ancient heathland under the driest, and bluest, skies in the country. Its human history goes back to the Stone Age when it was the flint factory of Britain, making some of the best tools available from its almost indestructible jet-black flint. Grime's Graves was one of just eleven Neolithic mines known in the British Isles, with over 400 shafts dug using antler picks to reach the flint seams some 13 metres (42 feet) beneath the sandy soils. The Anglo-Saxons reused the disused hollows of the mine, naming it after their god Grim. The Normans also reused Grime's Graves for the rabbits they introduced to the Brecks in the 12th century. Warrening became a major industry during the 16th and 17th centuries, with the output of some warrens exceeding 20,000 rabbits a year. Fur factories at Brandon processed the animals, providing meat to local markets, the Cambridge colleges and London.

Easy

1. Can you find three different colour names on the map, either as a word in themselves or as the start of another word?

2. Which are there more of marked on the map: nature reserves or camping and caravan sites?

Medium

3. Can you find the name of a two-wheeled handcart, as might be used by a street vendor?

4. Imagine drawing a barrier from north to south that joins the four 'building of historic interest' symbols in turn with straight lines. Which side of this barrier has the most museum symbols labelled: the west side or the east side?

Tricky

5. Where might you find a rearranged illegal hay void?

6. What single-word place sounds like a two-word phrase someone might have used to indicate they were not sick?

Challenging

7. Start at Thetford Station and travel two stops on the train westbound. Get off and follow the road so that you pass a mast on your right. Keep going until you reach a roundabout, then take the first exit. Joining the main road, head north to the edge of the map. How many walks or trails have you travelled directly past since joining the A road?

8. Imagine connecting the following places in the order given, forming one imaginary letter per set:
   - Eriswell > Hockwold cum Wilton > Weeting > Brandon Park > Wangford
   - Ickburgh > Santon Downham
   - Gazeley > Barton Mills > Burthorpe > Icklingham
   - Kilverstone Hall > Elveden > Brockley Corner > Fakenham Magna > Great Livermere
   - West Stow > Flempton > Fornham All Saints > Fornham St Genevieve > West Stow

What name for a natural feature, often found in Norfolk, have you spelled out?

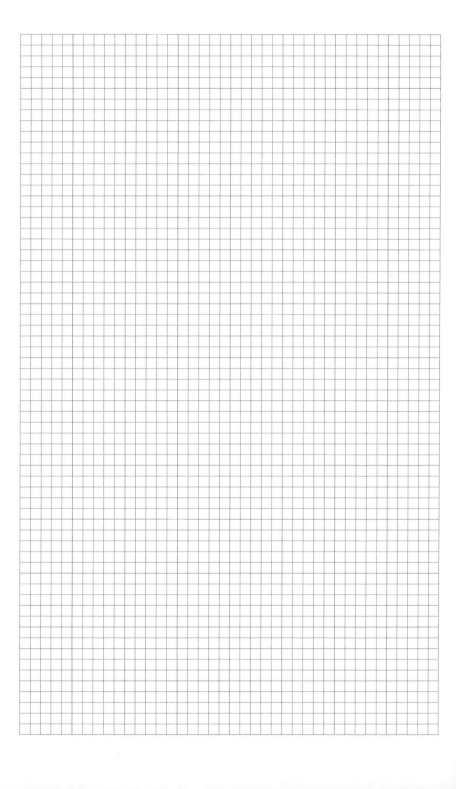

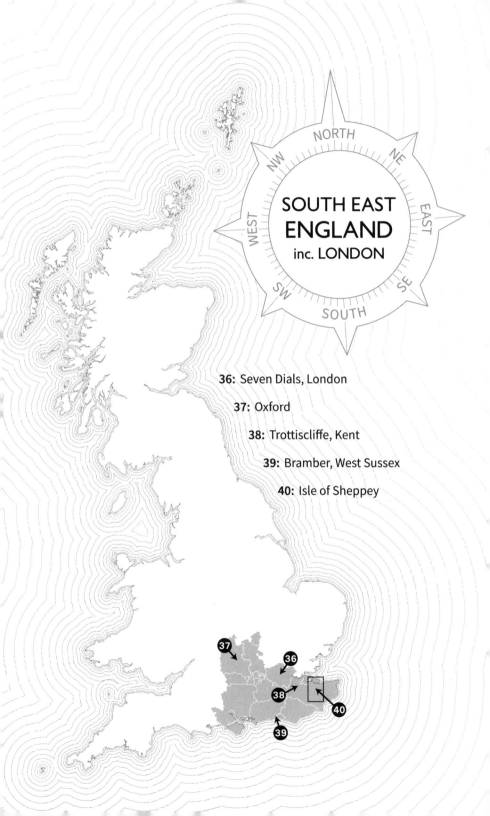

South East England inc. London

NORTH
NE
EAST
SE
SOUTH
SW
WEST
NW

SOUTH EAST
ENGLAND
inc. LONDON

GET OUTSIDE!

Name: Dan Raven-Ellison

Who are you?
I'm a guerrilla geographer and founder of the campaign to make London the world's first National Park City.

In three words, sum up what makes your area the best part of GB
London is diverse.

Your favourite walk
The Capital Ring, a 126-km (78-mile) circular walk around London.

Your favourite view
It's hard to pick one. The view from the Addington Hills viewpoint in Croydon across London is great. It's a good resting point if you're walking the London LOOP (the London Outer Orbital Path) too – a 242-km (150-mile) hike around the edge of Greater London!

Any local folklore?
'So long as the stone of Brutus is safe, so shall London flourish' is a saying that refers to the London Stone. This chunk of limestone was possibly brought to London by Brutus, the Roman who reputedly founded Britain. It's fortunately survived fire, flood and war and can today be found safely on display at 111 Cannon Street.

Describe the perfect day out in your area
Watch the sunrise from Parliament Hill then swim in one of Hampstead Heath's ponds. Grab some breakfast in Highgate then walk down Parkland Walk, a dismantled railway on the Capital Ring, to Finsbury Park. Enjoy an exhibition at Tate Modern and try to spot one of the resident peregrine falcons. Go stand-up paddle boarding from Kew Bridge, looking out for seals. Have some Vietnamese food in Soho, then go dancing.

Why people should visit
London is one of Earth's true hotpots of people, places, culture, wildlife and ideas, which makes it fascinating to explore. You might think you know London, but you don't. It's big, diverse, constantly changing.

MAP
36

BEST LAID PLANS

The map: OS London 1:1 056 (1895), colour tinted

The story: Urban planning, London

The MP Thomas Neale sought to build a desirable development near the successful Covent Garden Piazza in the early 1690s. His scheme divided up the area into triangles to maximise the rents he could charge, which at the time were calculated by the length of frontage and not by the area of the property's interior. The plan originally was for six roads and a sundial with six faces was commissioned for the central junction and installed early in the project before a seventh road was added to the plan. Many original buildings remain, although the road names have since been changed to avoid confusion with other London streets; Great and Little White Lion Streets are now an extension of Mercer Street, for example. Unfortunately, Seven Dials didn't remain a desirable address and became one of the more deprived areas of London with, at one point, seven pubs facing the centre. This improved as nearby areas developed and nowadays it is once again a fashionable place to shop, dine and live.

▧ Easy

1. At how many locations might a gentleman spend a penny?
2. How many words on the map describe European nationalities?

▧ Medium

3. If a full congregation of St Giles's Church were to attend a service at the Baptist Chapel, what percentage of them would have seats?
4. How many times does the word 'chapel' appear on the map?

▧ Tricky

5. Which residence block shares its name with the Queen's Norfolk estate?
6. Start at the junction of Shaftesbury Avenue, Great St Andrew Street and Neal Street. Travel along the tree-lined road until you reach a left turning with a pub ahead of you on a corner. Turn left, then immediately right. Continue along this road until you reach a complex junction of several roads. Follow the civil parish boundary left until you reach a crossroads, then turn left. When you reach the next junction, choose the road that will take you directly back to your starting point. How many fire hydrants have you passed on your route?

▧ Challenging

7. If you were ejected from the pub on New Compton Street and needed to find another pub, which would be the quickest to walk to?
8. Begin your route at a place where you might find someone young and hard up. From here, travel north-west along an ecclesiastical thoroughfare and climb the steps at the end of the road. Follow the winding path until you reach a place that might be useful if you were feeling parched. Head east as the crow flies to a building where you might find people talented at casting. Turn left out of this building, then take the first left, stopping at the fire hydrant. Which area is directly to your left?

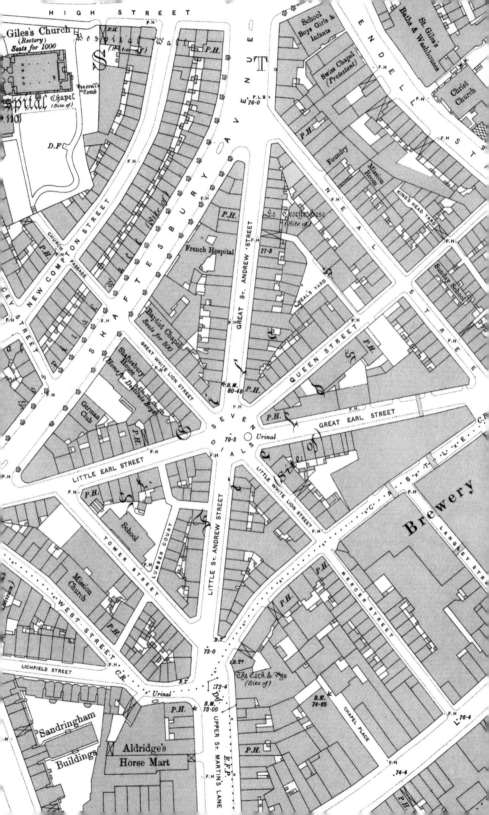

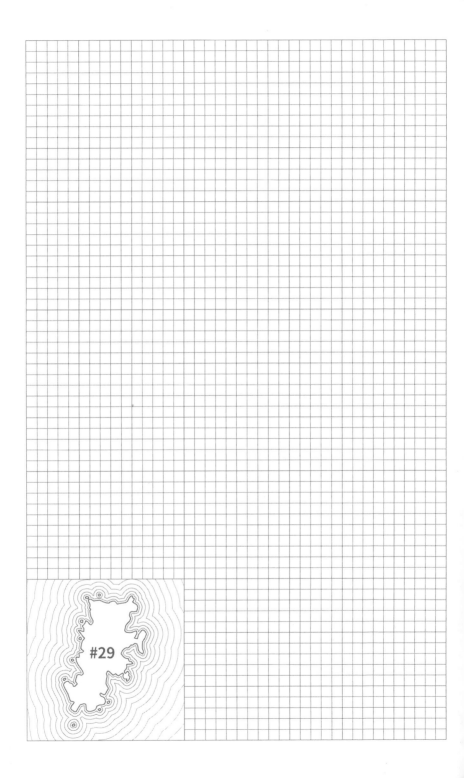

#29

MAP
37

BEATING THE BOUNDS

The map: Open Map Local Vector at 1:8 000 scale

The story: Walking the parish boundaries in Oxford

Historically, when the church fulfilled many of the welfare roles in society, the parish boundary played an important role defining the limits, and therefore the costs, that the parish church had to meet. Checking parish boundaries, knowing who lived within them and who didn't, was therefore an important task, traditionally carried out on Ascension Day by 'beating the bounds'. In Oxford the parishes of St Michael at the Northgate and St Mary the Virgin still perform this tradition with a procession around their boundaries, beating the various landmarks with willow wands, marking them with chalk and calling out, 'Mark! Mark! Mark!' Some boundary markers are now inside private properties and both parishes pass through Brasenose College. During the St Mary's walk, cherry cake is provided at All Souls College, which used to have a cherry orchard. The St Michael's walk ends at Lincoln College where a penance of ivy-flavoured beer is offered – remembering a time when Lincoln refused admittance to a Brasenose student who was then killed.

QUESTIONS

▨ Easy

1. How many places of worship are marked with symbols on the map?

2. How many street-name labels completely overlap with the parish boundaries drawn on the map?

▨ Medium

3. Which street name is also a driving instruction? And can you find a street on the map that sounds like it could describe the characteristics of a fast car?

4. What road shares its name with a small yellow bird in Charles M. Schultz's comic strip, Peanuts?

▨ Tricky

5. Find a tourist attraction whose symbol on the map is exactly 1 km from the symbol for Westgate Oxford, measuring as the crow flies. What is that attraction?

6. What is the fewest number of parish boundaries you have to cross to make your way from one coloured animal to another?

▨ Challenging

7. If there were two of this word on the map, there'd be joy. On its own, there's only sorrow. What is it?

8. Imagine connecting the numbered parish legend points with straight lines in increasing numerical order. How many complete (three-sided) triangles are formed?

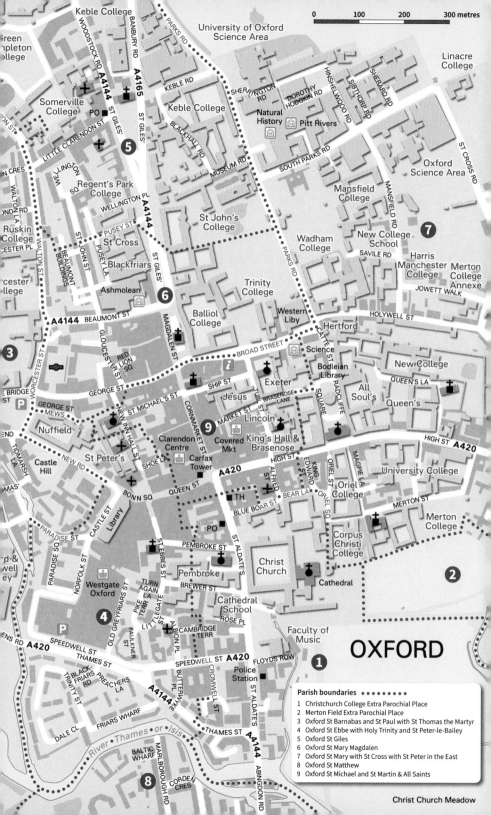

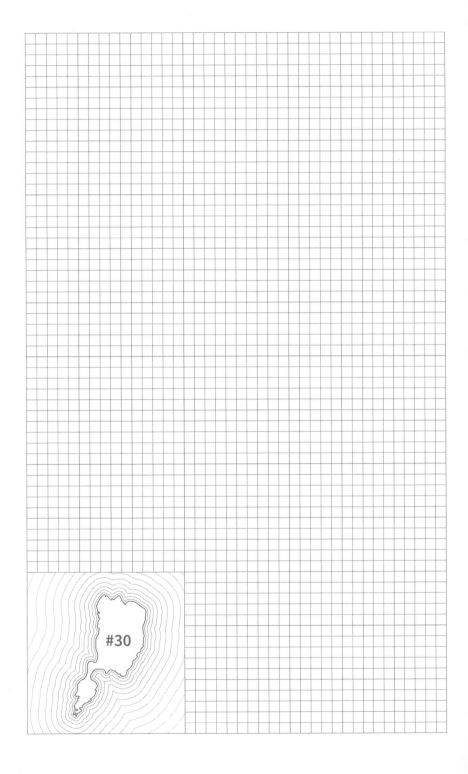

#30

SANDALS AND SACKCLOTH NOT COMPULSORY

The map: OS Explorer enlarged to 1:20 000 scale

The story: Ancient trackways

The trackways along the chalk ridges of southern Britain became established in the Neolithic period for trading purposes, providing easier travelling than the denser woodland, wetter marshes and sticky clays of the lowlands. Stonehenge, on the more open chalk downland to the west, became a destination, with trackways from the south east using the chalk escarpment of the North Downs. Before the Romans built their straight metalled roads, the trackways assisted travellers going north by linking the coast, through Canterbury, to a ferry crossing at London. Canterbury became a new focus after St Augustine became the first Archbishop of Canterbury in 597. Pilgrimages to Rome and to spiritual centres such as Canterbury and Winchester continued to use these ancient trackways and Roman roads. After the reformation in the 16th century, the veneration of saints fell away. Today we can enjoy these ancient routes as recreational paths with often stunning views.

Easy

1. How many places on the map have an animal in their name, either as a word in its own right or as the start or end of another word?

2. If you travel from the label for Vigo Village to the label for Ryarsh Wood as the crow flies, how many roads do you pass over?

Medium

3. Which place sounds like a good spot to grow seedlings?

4. There is a make of car on the map. What is it?

Tricky

5. Can you find some areas of open land that are having fun?

6. Start on what sounds like a clothes-maker's road. Travel east along a path fit for horses, then pass the church and cross the field on a route better suited to feet. Cross the road, jump back on your saddle and continue east, then turn right at the ancient site. Continue in a southerly direction until you reach an obstacle made of natural material. Where are you?

Challenging

7. What map feature links a symbolic lucky talisman and the name of a large waterbird?

8. Which words on the map do the following cryptic clues describe?
   a. Two vehicles surround one vehicle
   b. Tense stretcher, perhaps far to path

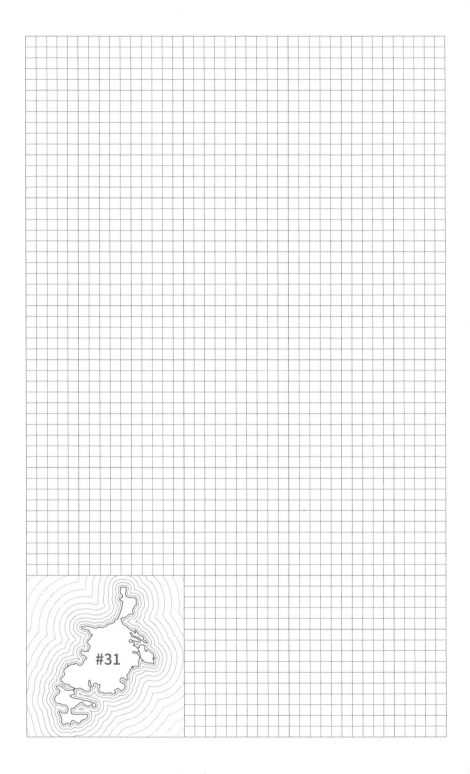

#31

MAP
39

A SOUTH DOWNS SQUEEZE

The map: OS Landranger enlarged to 1:40 000 scale

The story: Normans and the Sussex rapes

The origin of the Sussex rapes (county subdivisions) is unclear, but they were an early form of administrative unit similar to the neighbouring lathes of Kent. The Normans continued with the system after their conquest in the 11th century, adapting it to their needs and increasing the number of rapes from four to five. The rape of Arundel originally covered all of Sussex west of the River Adur, which also corresponded to the western area of the Sussex dialect. Bramber was added from parts of the Arundel and Lewes rapes to better defend the Adur estuary. Because the natural barrier of the South Downs is cut through by rivers that provided navigable access inland to small ships, the Normans built defensive castles at each of the inland ports. The rape of Chichester was added between 1250 and 1262 from the western half of Arundel rape. Each rape would hold an annual muster and had its own horse company. The administrative responsibilities of the rapes mostly disappeared by the end of the 19th century.

▨ Easy

1. What do the cemeteries, leisure centres and triangulation pillars shown on this map share in common?

2. How many bridges over the River Adur can you find?

▨ Medium

3. Which map label could be interpreted as a student radio station?

4. Can you find two places you might climb to grind grain, according to their names?

▨ Tricky

5. Which depression is lowest when dropped?

6. To the west of the river, can you find a line of equal height that crosses through the names of three farms? What are their names, and at what height do they all sit? Then can you find another three farms, only one of which is in common with the previous three farms that also share a line of equal height?

▨ Challenging

7. Subtract the sum of all the green road numbers (including duplicates) from the sum of all of the pink road numbers (but not the white on pink number). Divide your answer by 332. Where on the map can you find an elevation that matches this answer?

8. Starting on an incline that sounds like a decorative moulding, follow the regal route west past a fortified settlement. Continue until you reach a valley that sounds like a good basin for dyeing. If you look due east from here, what's the highest point you can see in the map area?

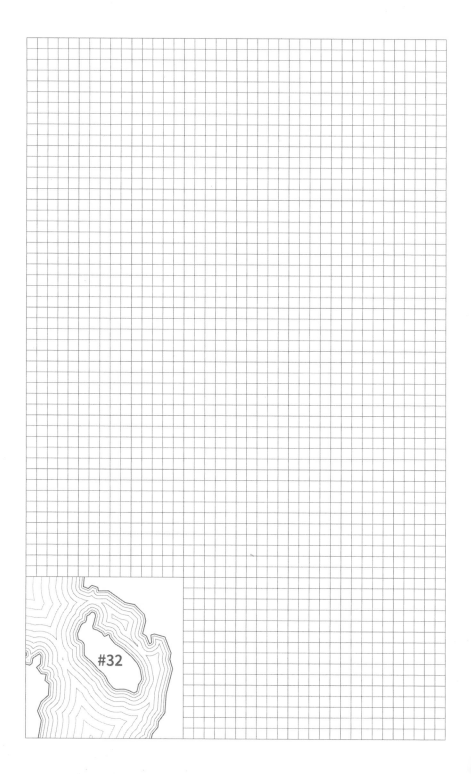
#32

MAP
40

INVADERS ASHORE!

The map: OS Road enlarged to 1:210 000 scale

The story: Sheep Island occupied

While this might be the last map in the book, the Isle of Sheppey (Old English 'Sceapig' or 'Sheep Island') was the starting point in southern Britain for the Vikings. The first recorded raid was in 835, where the monasteries around the island's low-lying coast were easy targets. By 855 the Vikings had an occupying force and the Kingdom of Kent had become part of Wessex, which eventually forced the Vikings out. King Henry VIII used the River Medway to anchor his naval ships and had a garrison fort built on the island to protect the entrance. By the 17th century, a Royal Navy dockyard was established at Sheerness by Samuel Pepys. Sheppey suffered the misfortune of being captured by a foreign power in 1667 when the Dutch navy attacked the port and overran the island for a few days before withdrawing – looting and burning as they left. It didn't help that the fort was incomplete at this time and the garrison poorly supplied and unpaid.

QUESTIONS

■ Easy

1. How many museums are marked on the map?

2. Which are there more of, 'garden or arboretum' symbols, or solar farms?

■ Medium

3. Can you find a place that might be identifying a purveyor of dairy products as being naïve?

4. Which town is 'floating up and down'?

■ Tricky

5. Can you identify these places?
   a. Somewhere recreational grounds might be grown
   b. A village you might use to season your chips

6. What might you say to a colleague who has just presented a high-quality graph?

■ Challenging

7. Can you use a ruler to find a straight line that passes through the first letter of three labels written in black text, with those labels starting in turn with the letters A, B and C as you follow the line? Then can you find three other straight lines that have the same property? (The lines may also pass through other labels too, but these are ignored. If a label consists of multiple words, only the first letter of the first word is considered.)

8. Start at the station which is the opposite of buying. Travel past a place to hear superstitions, head south-west on the National Trail, picking it up again after any settlements. Where it forks, take the path to your right and follow the devotees' route through a London train station without its cross. When you reach the star, what tourist attraction lies due west?

MASTER PUZZLE

You might think you've finished all of the puzzles in this book, but one challenge still awaits you. By cracking the code on this page, can you reveal an appropriate message?

31	40	9	14	21	36	13	1
5	4	7	4	2	5	5	3
4	2	3	3	5	2	3	2

7	32	24	17	30	1
3	5	8	6	3	7
2	6	1	6	1	2

6	33	2	34	29	16
3	4	3	3	4	5
4	2	3	2	5	10

5	25	27	38	3	35	23
6	2	4	5	7	8	5
2	2	4	5	2	3	3

22	12	37	4	20	15
4	6	4	8	5	4
3	2	6	3	3	1

26	10	28	1	19	8	39
5	4	4	4	6	4	5
1	3	2	4	2	2	2

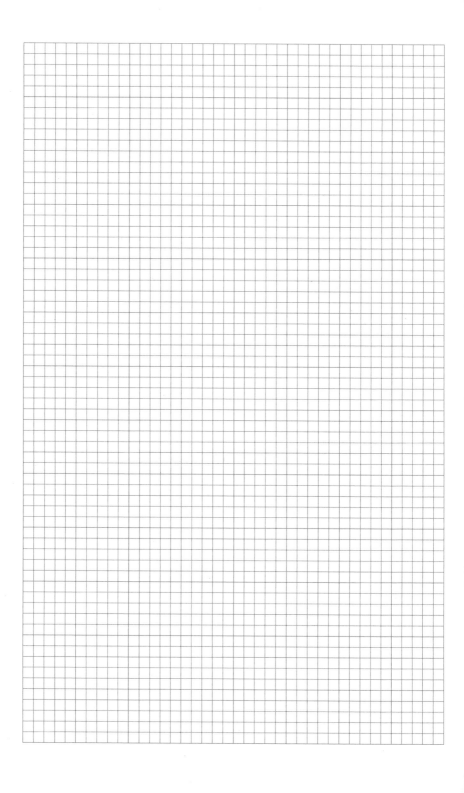

SOLUTIONS

MAP

1

1. Horse Rock, Shrimp Rock and Pig Rock

2. Eight

3. Giant's Castle

4. White Sheets

5. Normandy: begin at Great Britain Rock; head north to Deep Point; travel west to Carn Friars Lane; travel northwest to Normandy

6. Fish Pond: begin at B.M. 85.5; head south to Batteries; follow the 50-feet contour line to the edge of the green field area; head SSW along the footpath; you reach a narrow stretch of water connecting to Fish Pond

7. Twin Sisters: Jenna and Barbara Bush were twin sisters who were daughters of the 43rd US President, George W Bush

8.   a. Sun Rock
     b. Darrity's Hole
     c. Sir Cloudesley Shovel's Grave
     d. Higher Moors

MAP
2

1. 11: Parking, information centre, public toilets, theme park, preserved railway, beach, theatre, museum, hospital, shopping centre and nature reserve

2. Six: Rabling Lane, Manwell's Lane, Horsecliffe Lane, Mount Pleasant Lane, Cobblers Lane and Town Hall Lane

3. Cauldron Meadows

4. Bon Accord Road (from French)

5. There are four possible routes:

   • Head north on Queen's Road; cross onto Church Hill; cross onto Court Road; turn right onto Northbrook Road; turn left onto Walrond Road; arrive

   • Head north on Queen's Road; turn left onto High Street; turn right on Court Road; turn right onto Northbrook Road; turn left onto Walrond Road; arrive

   • Head north on Queen's Road; turn right onto High Street; turn left onto Institute Road; continue onto Shore Road; turn left onto Walrond Road; arrive

   • Head east on Queen's Road; turn left onto Taunton Road; continue straight onto Institute Road; continue onto Shore Road; turn left onto Walrond Road; arrive

6. HELP. The letters are:

   a. H: Travel down Queen's Road to the end of Mount Scar, then go back around the curve of Queen's Road to the hospital

   b. E: Travel along Victoria Avenue to Ilminster Road, then along Ilminster Road to Cranborne Road, then along the length of Cranborne Road and back, and then the remainder of Ilminster Road and the east half of Gilbert Road

   c. L: Travel along both parts of Manor Road

   d. P: Travel up along Newton Road, right along Queen's Road, south along Drummond Road and west along Salisbury Road

7. The words are:

   a. Square: found in 'The Square' – double definition

   b. Gilbert: found in 'Gilbert Road' – reference to Gilbert and Sullivan, and an anagram of 'girl' and 'bet'

8. Cauldron Crescent/Cauldron Barn Road/Cauldron Meadows and Cauldon Avenue

MAP
3

1. Just to the east of Dykes Farm, in the bottom half of the map

2. Six

3. Burrow Mump, as indicated by the 360-degree viewpoint symbol, and Mill Mound, as indicated by the contour lines

4. The Moat. Start at Parsonage Farm, travel west to Dykes Farm and join the road. Head west until you reach the Moat

5. RP Trail: 'RP' stands for Received Pronunciation, a standard pronunciation of British English

6. Turkey Cottage. Start at King Alfred's Monument, head southwest along the River Tone ('musical sound'), to Hook ('catch') Bridge. Head in a roughly northerly direction on the footpath (indicated with the green dashed line), away from the hill to the south east, until you reach Turkey Cottage

7. Normandy: the spot heights are 6, 6, 6, 7, 7, 8, 18, 21 and 21 for a total of 100

8. Pumping Station: the 'confused' (anagrammed) 'grubbier word' is Burrowbridge. Walk directly to Bull ('Taurean') Load Drove. A 90-degree turn will head you due west to the National Trail. The first utility on the opposite bank in a leftwards (south-westerly) direction is the Pumping Station

MAP
4

1. 529 metres, just south of Hookney Tor

2. Five: Bowden Farm, Gratnar Farm, Vogwell Farm, Grendon Farm and Hatchwell Farm

3. 15. However, there are two other named settlements found on the map: Foales Arrishes and Grimspound

4. Tumulus: with the first letter changed it can become cumulus

5. Moor Gate: Moorgate is a station on the Circle, Hammersmith & City, Metropolitan and Northern lines

6. Wind Tor (Winter) – located south of Widecombe in the Moor near the bottom of the map

7. 439 metres, as marked by the triangulation pillar at Easdon Tor. Start at Honeybag Tor, and travel north to the contour line marked 370. Then head east until you reach Jay's Grave. If you then travel due north you reach the triangulation pillar height that the crow must fly over

8. Grimspound. Starting at the place where four roads meet by the National Trust property at Widecombe in the Moor:
   a. Take the northwest road to the spot height of 312 metres by Lower Blackaton
   b. Travel south and onto the road that passes by the spot height of 286 metres
   c. Turn right at the four-way junction, passing Grendon Farm
   d. Continue almost straight, by turning right then left
   e. Travel north until you reach the bridleway, marked with a dashed pink line
   f. Just east of here is Grimspound, marked as an embankment as per the map key

MAP
5

1. 20: there are five nature reserves and four buildings of historical interest, and so 5 × 4 = 20

2. Badminton, north-east of junction 18 on the M4

3. Sheepscombe: without the final 'e', it can be read as sheep's comb – it is located near the top-right of the map, north-east of Stroud

4. 33 km

5. The routes spell out D, U, K and E, revealing the butterfly as the Duke of Burgundy

6. Slimbridge

7. a. Nailsworth
    b. Oldcroft Purton
    c. Thornbury
    d. Eastcombe
    e. Shurdington

8. Stone. The first letters of the solutions to question 7 spell NOTES, which can be rearranged to STONE. Stone is found just west of Michaelwood Services on the M5.

MAP
6

1. Two: there is one northwest of Oakeley Slate Quarries, and another just west of the Maen-Offeren label

2. Holland, in Holland View near the bottom of the map

3. Baltic Road and Baltic Hotel

4. Uncorn Terrace: this becomes 'unicorn' with the addition of an 'i'

5. 'Chap' (short for Chapel): there are five on the map. Note this is not a count of all chapels, since 'Ch.' is not counted, and buildings containing 'capel', the Welsh word for 'chapel', are also excluded

6. About 900 metres, which can be calculated using the scale at the top right of the map; and 500 metres. Pubs are labelled P.H., so the most easterly pub is just north-west of the Town Hall

7. The Methodist Chapel. Start at the reservoir next to the incline towards the top left of the map. The tramway is labelled just above the smithy. If you follow the path of the water, you will reach a benchmark number 743, and 4 + 3 = 7. If you follow the main road north from here, you reach the Methodist Chapel, labelled 'Meth. Chap.'

8. a. Waterfall: cascade ('waterfall') and 'after wall' anagrammed ('tumbled')
   b. Incline: slope ('incline') and 'in' + 'cli' (151 = CLI in Roman numerals) + 'ne' (compass points N and E)

MAP
7

1. Twice: Morgan Street and Clos Morgan

2. The most southerly three supermarkets, marked on the map as a blue shopping basket in a blue square

3. Coracle Way

4. Jolly Tar Lane

5. Pacman: this is found by removing an 'R' and 'E' from Parcmaen Street

6. Water Street/Little Water Street and Bridge Street/Little Bridge Street

7. Two: head out of the station and turn left onto the A484. Take a slight right onto Castle Hill, then turn right onto Spilman Street and follow the road around. Turn left onto St Peter's Street, where you will find the church entrance. As an alternative route, you could also travel via the A484, Old Station Road, Parade Road, Church Street and St Peter's Street

8. The Post Office. The three roads are Cae Crug, Cae Eithin and Cae Celyn, near the top centre of the map. Turn right from Cae Eithin and then left onto Brewery Road – beer is brewed with hops, so the road might 'smell like it'. Brewery Road turns into Waterloo Terrace, so the sixth right is a T-junction which takes you onto Heol y Sgubor/Narn Road. Next turn left onto John Street/Cambrian Place, where there is a church. Turning right takes you onto Chapel Street, where you will come to the junction with the Post Office

MAP

8

1. Eight: Gigrin Quarry, Stone Quarry (disused) and six unnamed disused quarries

2. Cycle hire and horse riding

3. Tumulus, a type of burial mound. A cairn is also marked on both maps, but only on the Dartmoor map are they labelled as ancient monuments

4. Pit, which becomes 'tip' when reversed – you might tip something into a pit

5. A mast. Your starting point is the point where the River Wye meets the Afon Elan. Follow the Wye until you reach the Tan House Bridge. Follow the smaller branch of the river, going under the Rhyd-hir Bridge. The stream that goes north crosses the 825 cycle route. There is a green dashed line marking a footpath which heads west, then continues on the other side of the B4518. If you walk along the footpath on the other side of the road, you will see a mast, just north of Coed-yr-ardd

6. Kite Feeding Centre: since a kite is both a toy and also a type of bird

7. Gwastedyn Hill, which contains 'wasted'

8. The A470. Start from the picture of the duck, and head south-east to the top of the hill. Head south to the ford, then west to the A470, near the Stone Quarry.

MAP
9

1. Six: Llanmadoc, Llanmadoc Hill, Llangennith Burrows, Llangennith Moors, Llangennith and Llwybr Arfordir Cymru

2. Four: Blue (Bluepool Corner), Green (Coety Green and Pilton Green), Red (Red Chamber), White (White Moor)

3. Five

4. Three: Druid, Monk and King, in Druids Moor/Druids Lodge, Monksland, Kingshall

5. Foxhole Point: head from the 51-metre point east of Kennexstone to a 49-metre point east of Old Henllys; travel to The Knave; go to Foxhole Slade, which has the same first word as Foxhole Point

6. a. Kimleymoor
   b. Culver Hole
   c. Tears Point

7. Minor Point (Pt)

8. Burry. The National Trust property with limited access has a white background rather than a purple one. Head north to the 193-metre triangulation pillar by The Beacon, and follow the (pink) bridleway to Burnt Mound. Head east to just north of Burry, then south to Burry itself

MAP
10

1. Five: Afon Cefni, Afon Dwyfor, Afon Dwyfach, Afon Glaslyn and Afon Menai

2. 40

3. Dutchman Bank

4. Carmel; it becomes 'caramel' if you add an 'a' to it

5. Three: B4418, A4085 and A4086

6. Nasareth – which needs just one letter changed to become Nazareth, where Jesus lived as a child according to the New Testament

7. Rhyd, Ynys and Crymlyn

8. 17.5 km: the 1461 battle site (symbolised by two crossed swords) can be found in Caernarfon and the highest peak is Snowdon/Yr Wyddfa, at 1085 metres

MAP
11

1. Denmark Road and Copenhagen Road

2. Eight

3. Botanic Street

4. Four: weighing machines are marked 'W.M.'

5. One: the Edge Hill Goods Station. The 'Crane' by the Railway Cottages would fly to the triangulation point just north of the Edge Hill Goods Station

6. Eight. Begin where Moorgate Street meets the tramlines at its northern end, near the middle of the map on the left. Passing three pubs will take you to Scourfield Street as the first left. Turn left into Crosfield Road and right into Grote Street. There are eight houses that face west on Grote Street

7. Speke Street and Wynne Street

8. B.M. (Benchmark) 171.1, east of Moorgate Street. The highest B.M. is 187.1 (found at the top of the map) and there are eight signal points (marked 'S.P.'), thus 187.1 – 16 = 171.1

MAP
12

1. There are in fact at least 14 different boys' names featured on the map: Peter Street, Thomas Street, St James' Road/James Street, St Stephen's Street, Robert Street, Albert Street, Cecil Street, Spencer Street, John Street, St Paul's Square, Duke Street, Byron Street, Earl Street and South George Street/St George's Crescent

2. Newmarket Road, Newark Terrace and Dukes Road. These can be found by the Sands Centre near the golf course

3. Seven: twice on Bridge Street; once over Eden Bridge and Nelson Bridge; on Junction Street; by the junction of Bridge Lane and Willow Holme Road; and at the end of Mayor's Drive

4. 700 metres: the bus station is marked in pink, and the most northerly museum is at the Castle

5. Citadel Row ('row' can also mean an argument)

6. Devonshire and Warwick: Devonshire Street/Devonshire Walk, Warwick Road/Warwick Street; there are also Milbourne Street/Milbourne Crescent and Court Square/Court Square Brow, although these are arguably not place names as required by the question

7. Three: Sheffield (Street), Lancaster (Street), Newcastle (Street)

8. Wet. The places are the Ski Centre ('slippery place'), Hadrian's Wall ('the barrier'), Cricket Ground ('insect park'), River Eden ('original flow-er' i.e. something that flows), Tennis Courts (where you might 'play a set'). The initials are SCHWCGRETC, thus the word is WET. Which you might be, if you swam the river

MAP
13

1. Six wind turbines and three masts (including one partially underneath a triangulation point by Hunger Hill)

2. Mount Etna

3. Cat Stones, near Pike Brow Quarry

4. Bone Hole

5. Little Ding

6. Lee Holme, which sounds like 'homely' when the words are reversed

7. An 'M': Marcroft Gate Farm > Knowl Hill > Rain Shore > Pike Brow > Bank House

8. Forsyth Brow. The heights are both 398 metres, so the water is just south of 'Bottom of Rooley Moor'. Due south is Shawfield Stones Farm, and north-west of here is the eastern side of Greenbooth Reservoir. The brook to the north points at Forsyth Brow

MAP 14

1. Five: they are marked 'LC', as per the map key

2. Four

3. Red: the map contains Red Hills (south of Arnside) and Red Bridge (east of Silverdale)

4. High Cote and Cote Stones

5. Three Brothers – found north of Warton

6. a. Slack Head
   b. Fairy Steps

7. 6 km: the highest point is the 163-metre spot point near Warton, and the viewpoint is marked by the National Trust property at the top left of the map

8. Silverdale Green. From Silverdale Station, head south on the yellow road and follow the green dots (cycle path) to the junction by Lindeth Twr. Turn right and head to where the pink diamond marks the National Trail. Follow it east then north until you reach Silverdale Green

MAP
15

1. High Street

2. Hutton (west of Penrith), Old Hutton (south-east of Kendal) and New Hutton (east of Kendal)

3. Crook, south-east of Windermere

4. Grizedale Forest: this is very similar to Grisedale Wood, north-west of Warton on Map 14

5. Whale and Scales

6. Shap Abbey. The named reservoir is Kentmere Reservoir. The high point is the spot height of 755 metres to the west. Travel to Helvellyn, and the 950-metre hill. Travel east to Shap Abbey

7. 321m. There are 17 telephones symbols inside this area. The lowest spot height is 116; the second lowest is 190. 190 + 17 = 207. There are 24 caravan/camping sites, 207 + 24 = 231. There is a spot height of 321 near the very bottom of the map

8. a. Askham – ask + ham
   b. Hartsop – hart + sop
   c. Mardale – mar + dale
   d. Dockray – dock + ray

MAP
16

1. Six: the Bridge of Tarff, the Swing Bridge, the Bridge of Oich and three bridges on the small river at the top left of the map

2. Six: three marked 'Mooring Posts', two marked 'M. Posts' and one marked 'M.P', just under the label for the northern pier

3. 1162: The highest number north of the river is 558 and the highest number to the south is 604

4. At the two manses (minister's houses) marked on the map, and at St. Benedict's Abbey

5. River Tarff: if you insert an 'i' you can obtain 'river tariff'

6. The Public Hall. The well is at the top right of the map. Head south-west and turn left from the junction at the end of the footpath to pass the smithy (where blacksmiths might have used an anvil), and then cross over the Bridge of Oich. Turning right will allow you to see both kinds of tree – they are labelled with different symbols on the map. The first building complex on your right is the Public Hall

7. Roughly six minutes. The distance on the map is approximately 10–11 cm, giving a distance of about 500 metres by using the printed scale. At 5 km/h, this would take you six minutes

8. a. Locks, Pier
   b. School, Hotel
   c. Pavilion, Cistern
   d. Manse, Boat House

MAP
17

1. Neither: there are ten norths and ten souths (although there is also 'Northumberland', but that is not the word 'north')

2. Ten

3. Take your pick from these seven: Old Town, Old Fishmarket Close, University of Edinburgh Old College, Old College, Elder Street, New Town, New College

4. Lawnmarket and Grassmarket

5. 900 metres (or, more precisely, 925 metres). The most northerly church with a spire is on George Street and the leisure location that suggests pandemonium is Bedlam

6. Bristo Square/Bristo Place, which would become Bristol if you added an 'L'

7. Turn onto the unnamed yellow road behind the hospital, cross to Lady Lawson Street, turn onto Castle Terrace, which becomes Johnston Terrace, and then onto Castlehill

8. York Place tram stop. Hanover is a city in Lower Saxony, and from Hanover Street you can travel east through Thistle Street (national flower of Scotland) to St David Street. Head north onto Queen Street, and pass along York Place (Jorvik being the source of the name 'York') to York Place tram stop

MAP
18

1. This can be found immediately east of the museum symbol by North Pier

2. Four caves, eight places of worship (three with a cross, two cathedrals, two churches with a tower, and one place of worship with a spire, minaret or dome)

3. Pulpit Hill

4. Tom nan Gobhar

5. 60. Start at the caravan site by Ganavan Bay at the top of the map, head south on the orange road until you reach the pink road. Turn left and right, and follow the A85 until you turn onto the A816. Diverge onto the orange road to the east by the Post Office (PO) and travel to where it degrades to a yellow road. The heights passed are 12, 6, 11, 5, 5, 4 and 17

6. NTL: NTL Incorporated was a cable company that offered customers television, internet and telephone services. NTL stands for 'Normal Tide Limit' on OS maps

7. Hill: Cnoc Poll a'Mhinisteir and Cnoc Càrnach both have rounded contour lines and high elevations

8. a. Michael's Rock: Carraig Mhìcheil
   b. Large Marsh: Lòn Mòr
   c. Black Lake: Lochan Dubh
   d. Large Ridge: Druim Mòr

For further information on Gaelic words on OS maps, visit:
www.ordnancesurvey.co.uk/resources/historical-map-resources/gaelic-placenames.html

MAP
19

1. The masts are in the top left corner of the map, at Saxa Vord. This is a high point on the map, so a great place to ensure a clear signal to other locations in the area

2. Seven: Cairns, Church (rems of), Chapel, Cairn, Cross Kirk (rems of), Chambered Cairns, and Broch (rems of)

3. The building by Sothers Field, as is made clear by the contour lines

4. Boat Haven

5. About 3.6 km: the triangulation pillar is on the east coast, by Hagmark Satck, while the National Trust for Scotland site is in the south, at Swinna Ness

6. Balta: if the first letter is changed it could become Malta

7. The Church near Kirkaton. Start at the cave just north of Grisa Lee, then travel east to the small lake labelled Loomer Shun. From the lake, take the second left through Sothers Field, then the second right past the Ward of Norwick to the yellow road. The T-junction is just north of The Cliffs – if you turn right here and follow the white road south along the coast, taking a left and then an immediate right onto the yellow road, you come to Kirkaton

8. Four. Start at Athans and travel to Burgar – these are plausible misspellings of 'Athens' and 'burger'. En route, you pass Mooa Stack, Hinda Stack, Hagmark Stack and Ship Stack

MAP
20

1. Ten: Moniack Castle is near the bottom left of the map, and walks or trails are indicated by blue footprints

2. Six: Easter Fearn Burn (a river), Easter Ardross, Easter Kinkell, Easter Suddie, Easter Moniack and the large label Easter Ross

3. Pollo: this is located north of Invergordon

4. Mount Eagle: an eyrie is an eagle's nest

5. Monument (west of Alness). Start at the battle site marked 1746 south of Balloch. Travel north to the active lighthouse on Chanonry Point. Follow the coast north to Blue Hd viewpoint, then fly west to the camping and caravan site at Culcairn. Just north of you is the Monument viewpoint

6. 2.5 km shorter. There is one service station (marked with a white 'S' in a black diamond) near Alness and another (marked with a black 'S' in a white diamond) at Tore. It is roughly 18 km by road, and about 15.5 km as the crow flies

7. Newton and Milton are neighbouring settlements at the west end of Beauly Firth. Isaac Newton discovered gravity after watching a falling apple, and John Milton wrote Paradise Lost about Eve eating the apple in the garden of Eden

8. Navity: if 'it' came back(wards) inside it, you would get Nativity

MAP
21

1. Six: one by the bottom building marked 'Laundry', two in and around the Electricity Generating Station and three in the Gas Works in the top half of the map

2. Layerthorpe Bridge, and southwards. Using the benchmarks, where the arrows point to the precise point where the OS benchmarks are, Monk Bridge has an elevation of 38.2 feet, whereas Layerthorpe Bridge has an elevation of 40.9 feet. Meanwhile, the arrow in the middle of the river near the top of the map shows the direction of flow

3. Downhill Street

4. John Bull (Yard)

5. 31.3 feet – from the 48.7 benchmark, head northwest to the upper end of Foss Bank, and along it to the 31.3 benchmark

6. Vicars Row

7. O. This sentence requires some interpretation. The path is: Allotment ('a lot meant': Allotment Gardens) to Chapel ('chap L', at the top left of the map), to Wall ('war L', written in a Gothic font lower down on the left), to Cross (Cross Court, on right of map) and back up to Gardens (Allotment Gardens, where you began). This traces a rectangle, which of the three largest letters visible on the map – M, O and N – most approximates the O

8. Refuse [the] Destructor (simple, really!)

MAP
22

1. Four: Chancery Lane, Tammy Hall Street, Union Street (the northernmost label, east of the bus station) and Walker's Terrace

2. Seven: Back Lane, Westgate, Ings Road (twice), Denby Dale Road, Kirkgate, Waldorf Way and Thornes Lane (twice)

3. Fox Way. Starting at Lady La[ne] just south of Ings Road, turn right onto George Street, then left onto Market Street. Follow Westgate onto Kirkgate, continuing as it becomes the A61, then joining the A638 Ings Road westwards. Turn left onto the A636 (Denby Dale Road), then onto Waldorf Way, and finally Fox Way

4. Bull Ring

5. Turner Way: it sounds like 'turn away'

6. You have formed the letter 'Z', which only appears in Zetland Street, towards the top right of the map

7. Approximately 830 metres – the place with spines and leaves is the Library; the 'narrow brimmed hat' refers to Trilby Street, and the aristocrat is Earl Street, while the place they meet is the point at the top right of the map where they intersect

8. Burgage Square: burgage was a type of tenure in which land or property was held in return for a service or an annual rent

MAP
23

1. 29: four labelled 'Sprs', 24 labelled 'Spr', and one labelled '(Spring)'

2. Hang Gliding Site: marked at the top right of the map

3. The northern direction is likely to be gentler, given the steepness of the climb at the south-west corner of the map

4. Pike Hill

5. East End, near Gayle. The letter created by joining these points is an 'E'

6. Nine times: there are six lows, including one in 'Bellow', and three highs

7. About 45 minutes: the distance along the river on the map is roughly 11.5 cm, giving a total distance of about 2.3 km at the map scale of 1:20 000

8. a. Thorns: tense 't' (dictionary abbreviation) + horns = thorns
   b. Gayle: woman (Gayle) sounds like ('heard in') a storm, gale

MAP
24

1. The 👓 marking can be found west of Middleton Old Town at the bottom of the map

2. 1402: found east of Bendor along the A697

3. Happy Valley: the 326-metre label is by Hart Heugh, and the steepest edge of the hill takes you to Carey Burn. Follow it east to the yellow road, and then north-east to the phone box

4. 3.4 km: on-road cycle routes are marked with green dots, so the two bridges are by Coldgate Mill and in Wooler by the weir

5. 323.67 metres – averaged from 200 metres at Dod Law, 319 metres at Gains Law, and 452 metres at Cold Law

6. Five: there are five 'MP's on the map (actually mileposts)

7. a. Coronation Wood
   b. Tower Martin
   c. Watch Hill

8. Cairns, east of Fredden Hill. Start at Noble Lands (noble being a description of having honourable principles), and head to Doddington Bridge (a crossing). Fly west to East Wood, and head south to the coniferous wood by Coldberry Hill. Head south to the Cairns

MAP
25

1. 13

2. Hawnby

3. White Horse: this large carving in the hillside can be seen from the
    A road below

4. Nunnington. Starting at the youth hostel, shown as a pink triangle, head
    north to the phone, west to the phone, and south along the river to the
    Hall by Nunnington

5. a. River Dove – doves are a sign of peace
    b. Boosbeck – boos + beck (stream)
    c. Fangdale Beck – fang + dale + stream

6. The station at Commondale. Starting at the spot height of 454 metres in the
    middle of the map, travel along the green dashed line east, and follow it
    as it turns north. Enter the white road by the Battersby label and turn right
    onto the yellow road. Continue to Commondale. The place to 'board' is not
    a hotel, but the train station

7. Approximately 31 km: the places are Commondale (common + dale) and
    Felixkirk – 'felix' is Latin for lucky, and 'kirk' is a Scottish word for church

8. a. Tanton
    b. Little Ayton
    c. Rudland Rigg
    d. Arden Great Moor

MAP
26

1. Thorn Road

2. Camp Wood: found in the upper half of the map near the corner of Acacia Road and Maple Road

3. Oxford Street, Regent Street and Bond Street. These can be found east of the Worcester & Birmingham Canal

4. Acacia Road and Laburnum Road

5. Brick Works: starting at the northernmost triangulation pillar ('524'), draw a straight line to the island in the middle of the Fish Pond, travel east to Oxford Street, draw a line back up to the Brick Works building

6. 'The': of The Bourn, directly beneath Bournville Works

7. The Dell: Southampton F.C.'s former ground

8. a. Elan Aqueduct
   b. Engine Shed
   c. Ammunition Works

MAP
27

1. Curzon Street/Curzon Place

2. Clinton and Lincoln: Clinton Street E/Clinton Street W and Lincoln Street

3. St Peter's Gate

4. Victoria Street: this shares its first words with the intu Victoria Centre

5. Hollow Stone. Take the tram to Royal Centre Tram Stop, then head up Goldsmith St, turning right onto Talbot St. Turn left onto South Sherwood St, then travel along Shakespeare Street and turn right onto Milton Street. Head south, then east along Pelham Street and Carlton Street. Turn onto Stoney Street and eventually onto Hollow Stone

6. Weekday Cross

7. Barker Gate. Start in Hounds Gate. There are two Hounds Gates, but the most westerly is immediately north-east of the castle. Follow Castle Road to Castle Boulevard (A6005). Adding three to A6005 leads you to the A6008, Canal Street. Go along Canal Street to Middle Hill and continue as it turns to Weekday Cross and Fletcher Gate, then turn onto Warser Gate (opposite Bottle Lane – a 'container'). Turn right onto Stoney Street opposite Woolpack Lane, then onto Barker Gate. A dog could be a 'barker', and you started on a 'Gate' street

8. Old Street. Start at Kent Street, as Kent is often called 'the garden of England'. From here, travelling north-west takes you over Rick Street and Howard Street to Perth Street – Perth is a location in both Scotland and Australia. Perth Street is adjacent to Old Street, also a London station on the Northern line

MAP
28

1. There are five historical sites: Grind Low, Tumulus, Medieval Village (site of), another Tumulus and Cairn Circle

2. White House Farm

3. The Map Plantation

4. Wigger Dale. Start at the footbridge on the River Lathkill south of Over Haddon, then head to Raper Lodge. Exit on the north bank of the river, and follow the long-dashed green line. Travel on this bridleway north until you join the orange road, and follow the dark dotted line eastwards by Noton Barn Farm. Follow it to Wigger Dale

5. Coalpit Lane – when the 'p' is changed to a 't', it becomes 'coaltit'

6. About 2.3 km. It is roughly 11.5 cm from Baltic Wood to Ditch Cliff on the map, giving a total distance of 2.3 km, based on a map scale of 1:20,000

7. You have written the initials BT, the initials of Bakewell tarts. This is associated with the town of Bakewell, located just north of the area covered by the map

8. They all start with the letter 'H':
   a. Haddon – had + don
   b. Harthill – hart + hill
   c. Hopping – hop + ping

MAP
29

1. 12 (not including Old Man's Head Spring)

2. Middle Street

3. Ascend: the two Romans are the Roman roads, and the stoat's coat is Ermine Street. Whether you head north or south from the point where the two roads meet, you will go up in elevation by the edge of the map

4. Welton Cliff. Travel from the B1398 onto the A1500 as far as the orange contour line crossing the Horncastle Lane label. Due north of here is Welton Cliff

5. 6.5 km: the distance from the moat in Cammeringham to the rectangle of water surrounded by embankments near to Fox Covert

6. 3. The sum of the road numbers is 15 + 46 + 1398 + 1500 = 2,959; the sum of the spot heights adjacent to the B1398 is 21 + 23 + 27 + 48 + 49 + 56 + 69 = 293. Three is the only digit in the second answer that does not appear in the first

7. Heathcliff. The points of the triangle are the four crosses signalling places of worship to the south-east of the airfield; West Hall, which lies on the eastern side of the map; and Home Farm. Within this triangle are Heath Lane and Welton Cliff, which together contain the two halves of the name Heathcliff, a character in *Wuthering Heights*

8. a. Oil Well
   b. Scampton
   c. Brattleby
   d. South Carlton
   e. Burton-by-Lincoln

MAP
30

1. Seven: including the 360° viewpoint on the Wrekin just south of Wellington

2. Five: in Cound Brook, Coalbrookdale, Marshbrook, Rea Brook, Borle Brook

3. Middleton, which is just to the north-west of Henley, near Ludlow

4. The mast at a 540-metre elevation on Brown Clee Hill

5. A public telephone. Start at Homer, and travel south on the A4169, which becomes the B4378, until you pass Presthope and Easthope (ending in hope, i.e. optimism). Drive past Weston and stagger across onto the white road the ends at the public telephone

6. Four: they are marked by the grey square depicting the sun shining behind a solar panel, all found towards the top of the map

7. Shrewsbury. Start at Elton (John) in the bottom left of the map, and head to the castle (rook) in Ludlow. Travel east to Hints (clues), then to (Lily) Savage (paired with Neen, a palindrome). Go due north to Trench (top of map), then head to (Tony) Hadley nearby. Board the train in Wellington, and travel to Shrewsbury.

8. a Horsehay – horse + hay
   b. Buildwas – build + was
   c. Wilderhope (Manor) – wilder + hope
   d. Stapleton – staple + ton

MAP
31

1. Four: one at the top left above Fisher Fleet, one at the bottom left, one near the Saw Mills, and one in Alexandra Dock. The word 'Staithe', in Common Staithe Quay, might arguably also be counted, since 'staithe' also indicates a landing stage

2. 15

3. Water Lane

4. St Nicholas' Street

5. The Corn Exchange. Head west from Surrey Street, then north to the west end of Market Lane. Across the 'place' (the Market Place) is the Corn Exchange

6. a. Swing Bridge
   b. Landing Stage
   c. St. Ann's Fort

7. The Baths: start at the Globe Hotel (referencing the Globe Theatre), and travel to the pub, marked P.H. in the north-eastern corner of Tuesday Market Place. From here, head through the buildings towards the Saw Mills label. At the rail crossroad on the south-west corner of Alexandra Dock, turn right until you reach a benchmark of 20.3. Then move to the 19.3 benchmark, located in the bottom-left corner of the map near Water Lane. The Fire Engine House and Corn Exchange have already been referenced in other answers

8. a. Subway: sub (sandwich) way (street)
   b. Market: mark (label) ET (alien)
   c. Landing: LAN (network) ding (chime)
   d. Mooring: moo (low) ring (peal)

MAP
32

1. Six. Places of worship are denoted by a black cross; those that have a tower or spire, minaret or dome have either a black square or black circle below the cross

2. Short Cut Road

3. Londinium (Road) – Londinium was the Roman name for London

4. Head Gate

5. Serpentine Walk

6. Wakefield Close: it sounds like 'wake field'

7. Sir Isaac's Walk: i.e. Sir Isaac Newton

8. The library. Form an arrow by drawing a line from Roman Circus Walk at the bottom left of the map through the multistorey car park to Sir Isaac's Walk, then to Corporal Close (bottom right of map), then to St John's Green Primary School, then back to the starting point. This makes an arrow pointing north

MAP
33

1. St Theobald's Church, the Castle and Horstead Mill

2. 24 metres: by the water tower, labelled as 'W Twr'

3. 27: there are spot heights of 6 metres, 4 metres and 12 metres, and a contour height of 5 metres

4. Doctor's Cut

5. High Banks

6. Potspoon Hole. The reservoir is south-east of Horstead, labelled 'Resr'. From here, follow the B1150 north, then join the yellow road passing Ling Common. The footpath on the right, marked with green dashes, takes you to a wooded area by Potspoon Hole

7. A fish (the symbol for a fishing pond). The line would start at 'Paradise' at the bottom right of the map, then pass through 'Limit of Navigation' (in the centre) en route

8. 2.2 km. The starting point is the spot height number 17, south of three quadrilateral lakes. Travel south-east to Little Switzerland, then join the bridleway by High and Low Bridge. Follow this north, head up the yellow road and turn right onto the bridleway by Heggatt Hall. The path forks just north of the Heath. From here, it is approximately 10.8 cm back to the spot height, and since the map scale is 1:20 000 then the distance is about 2.2 km

MAP
34

1. a. Two cemeteries (Cemy): west of Leiston and just south of Eastbridge
   b. Two museums (Mus): top right of the map and in the middle of Leiston at the bottom of the map
   c. Two masts: to the left of Leiston Abbey and northwest of Leiston Common

2. They are noted by the abbreviation 'Twr', as per the legend at the start of the book. These can found to the east of the Power Station

3. Broom Hill

4. The public house and forestry commission site. There is 3.8 km between beacons (on Minsmere Cliffs and Goose Hill), since the distance on the physical map is 9.4 cm, and the scale is 1:40 000. The distance between the most westerly public house (in Theberton) and most easterly forestry commission site (marked by a symbol of two trees by Dunwich Cliffs) is approximately 5.5 km

5. The Cupola, which features seven windows facing out of the space station

6. 116: the different numbers are 1, 3, 6, 9, 11, 19, 21, 22 and 24

7. Scott's Hall. The glasshouse is at the bottom of the map, south-east of Buckle's Wood. Head east to the level crossing ('LC'). Turn left onto Abbey Rd, until you reach Theberton church. Take the yellow road past Rattla Corner, and turn left and head to Eastbridge. Turn left onto the road with on-road cycle route (green solid circles), and then east onto the National Trail (pink diamonds). Follow the National Trail until the junction with the footpath (pink dashes) to the left, and head south to Scott's Hall

8. a. Ash Wood (type of tree + golf club)
   b. Spring Covert (season of the year + word meaning 'undercover')
   c. Sizewell Belts (the name of a power station + a type of 'constraints')

MAP
35

1. The colours are red, black and green, found in Red Lodge, Blackthorpe, and Thistley Green, Broad Green, Dunstall Green, Lady's Green, Timworth Green or Rougham Green

2. There are the same number of each: five

3. Barrow

4. The east side, which has three museums; the west side has two

5. Holiday Village – it is an anagram ('rearranged') of 'illegal hay void'

6. Feltwell – it sounds like 'felt well'

7. Two. If you travel two stops westbound from Thetford station, you reach Lakenheath station. From here, travel south, passing a mast on your right. The roundabout is by The Delph, take the first exit to the A 1065. Travelling north, there are two footprint icons directly next to the road which indicate a walk or a trail

8. PINGO. Pingos are small ponds or lakes which were created around 20,000 years ago, when ice formed under the soil, creating small hillocks. These subsequently collapsed as the ice receded, leaving depressions that fill with water. Many of these can be found in Norfolk

MAP
36

1. Two: at the street urinals on Great Earl Street and West Street

2. Three: Swiss Chapel, French Hospital and German Club

3. 50 per cent – there are 500 seats in the Baptist Chapel and 1000 in St Giles's Church

4. Four: in Swiss Chapel, Baptist Chapel, Chapel Place and Chapel (site of)

5. Sandringham Buildings

6. Eleven. Shaftesbury Avenue is lined with trees, so walk south-west along it here and take a sharp left onto Little Earl Street, then turn right onto Tower Street. At the junction at its end, follow the black dotted line indicating the civil parish boundary to the crossroads. Turn left onto Little White Lion Street, then at the Seven Dials junction head north along Great St Andrew Street to where you started. You have passed eleven fire hydrants, labelled 'F.H'

7. The pub – notated as PH for 'public house' – on the corner of Great St Andrew Street and Queen Street would be the closest to walk to, even though it is not the closest as the crow flies

8. King's Head Yard. The starting point is Shaftesbury House – it is labelled as a 'home for destitute boys'. From here, head up Church Passage (an ecclesiastical thoroughfare) then up the steps to the white space south of St Giles's Church. The place that may help with feeling parched is the drinking fountain, marked D.F. From here, the first labelled building due east is the Foundry, a building where metal casting takes place. Turning left onto Neal Street then left again takes you to a fire hydrant directly opposite King's Head Yard

MAP
37

1. 18

2. Ten: the boundaries are marked in pink, and completely overlapping street-name labels are entirely in pink

3. Turn Again Lane and Speedwell Street – it sounds like 'speed well'

4. Woodstock Road

5. The Natural History Museum

6. One. To travel from Red Lion Square to Blue Boar Street, you need to pass from Oxford St Mary Magdalen parish into Oxford St Michael and St Martin & All Saints parish. Part of Blue Boar Street forms the border between this parish and Christchurch College Extra Parochial Place parish, but if you don't cross this boundary then you will have crossed only one parish boundary

7. Magpie (Lane), next to Oriel College. The question is referring to the rhyme about magpies that starts: 'One for sorrow, Two for joy, Three for a girl, Four for a boy'

8. Two

MAP
38

1. Five: Goose Farm, Sparrowhaugh Farm, Swansword Farm, Tiger's Hall Farm and Whitehorse Wood

2. Four: two orange and two yellow roads

3. Nursery: just to the west of Vigo Village

4. Ford (Lane)

5. Playing Fields: fields (areas of open land) are playing (having fun)

6. Woodgate. Taylor's Lane (clothes-maker's road) near Trottiscliffe has a bridleway (fit for horses) heading east. Follow this, past where it becomes a footpath and then a bridleway again, and turn right after Long Barrow (the ancient site). Follow the trail to Woodgate – an 'obstacle made of natural material' ('wood gate')

7. A contour line at a height of 175 metres. The symbolic lucky talisman refers to the horseshoe symbol (indicating horse riding) at the top right of the map, and the large waterbird is the Goose in Goose Farm at the top left of the map. Both labels are intersected by 175-metre contour lines

8. a. Caravan: two vehicles ('car' and 'van') surround one ('a') to make another vehicle ('caravan')

   b. Trackway: tense is 't' (dictionary abbreviation), stretcher perhaps is 'rack' (as in a medieval 'stretcher'), far is 'way' (as in 'far better' being equivalent to 'way better'), and a trackway is a type of path

MAP
39

1. There are two of each of them

2. There are nine bridges that cross the River Adur, not including bridges over the tributary just below Brighton City Airport

3. College Fm (although in reality 'Fm' is an abbreviation for farm, not FM)

4. Windmill Hill and Mill Hill

5. Anchor Bottom

6. The names of Upper Maudlin Farm, Annington Farm and Titch Hill Farm are all intersected by the same 50-metre contour line. You can also find the Farm Attraction crossing this contour line. In addition, the names of Poultry Farm, Annington Farm and Applesham Farm are all crossed by the same 30m contour line

7. The 12-metre spot height at the top left corner of the map, by Poultry Farm and Staplefields. The pink road numbers are 2025 + 259 + 283 + 2037 = 4604, and the green road numbers are 27 + 27 + 283 + 283 = 620. Then 4604 – 620 = 3984, and 3984 ÷ 332 = 12

8. Beeding Hill, with a spot height of 169 metres. The route also starts at Beeding Hill (sounds like 'beading') and follows the Monarch's Way (regal route) past Castle Town (the 'fortified settlement'). It continues along the Monarch's Way to Steyning Bowl (sounds like 'staining bowl')

MAP
40

1. 11

2. Gardens or arboretums: there are five solar farms (grey square sun/panel symbol) and six gardens or arboretums (blue flower symbol)

3. Cheeseman's Green

4. Bobbing

5. a. Park Farm b. Seasalter

6. Great Chart

7. The four possible lines are:
   a. Abbey > Borden > Castle
   b. Abbey > Boughton Malherbe > Curteis' Corner
   c. Abbey > Belmont > Challock
   d. Aldington Frith > Brook > Crundale

8. A castle. Start at Selling station (the opposite of buying) and travel south along the tracks until you reach Old Wives Lees (a place to hear superstitions) then join the footpath . The footpath forks and becomes Pilgrim's Way (the devotees' route) and passes through Charing (as in London's Charing Cross station). Due west of the tourist attraction marked by the star is the Castle

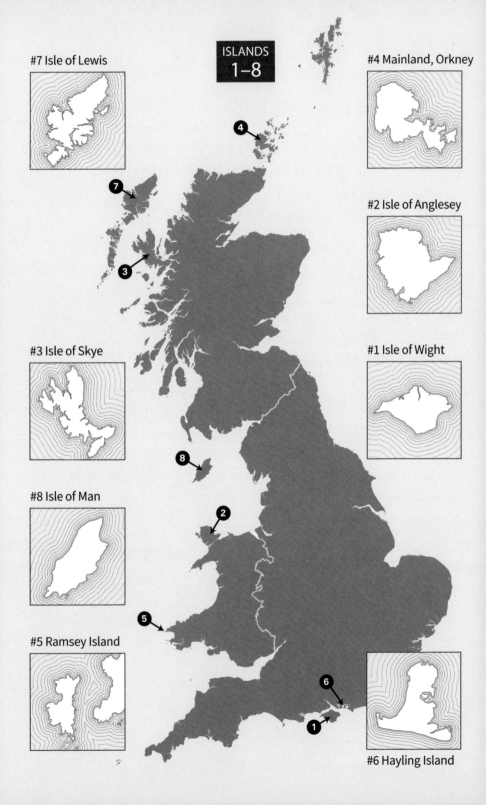

ISLANDS
1–8

#7 Isle of Lewis

#4 Mainland, Orkney

#2 Isle of Anglesey

#3 Isle of Skye

#1 Isle of Wight

#8 Isle of Man

#5 Ramsey Island

#6 Hayling Island

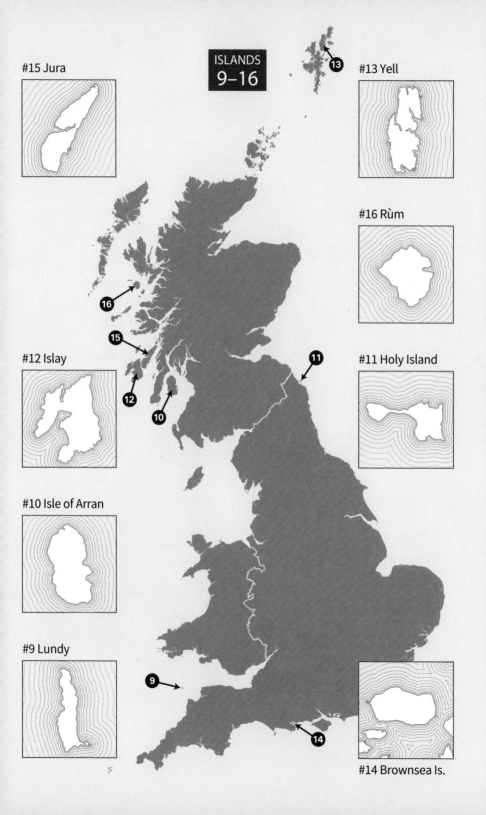

ISLANDS
9–16

#15 Jura

#13 Yell

#16 Rùm

#12 Islay

#11 Holy Island

#10 Isle of Arran

#9 Lundy

#14 Brownsea Is.

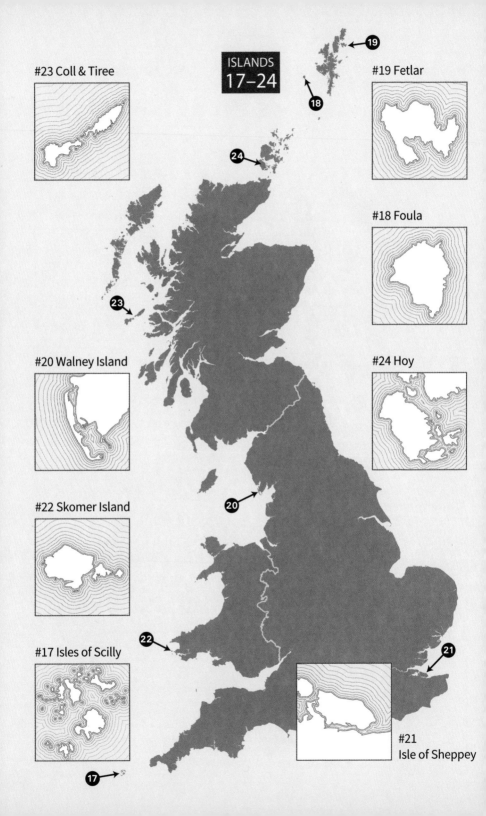

ISLANDS 17–24

#23 Coll & Tiree

#19 Fetlar

#18 Foula

#20 Walney Island

#24 Hoy

#22 Skomer Island

#17 Isles of Scilly

#21 Isle of Sheppey

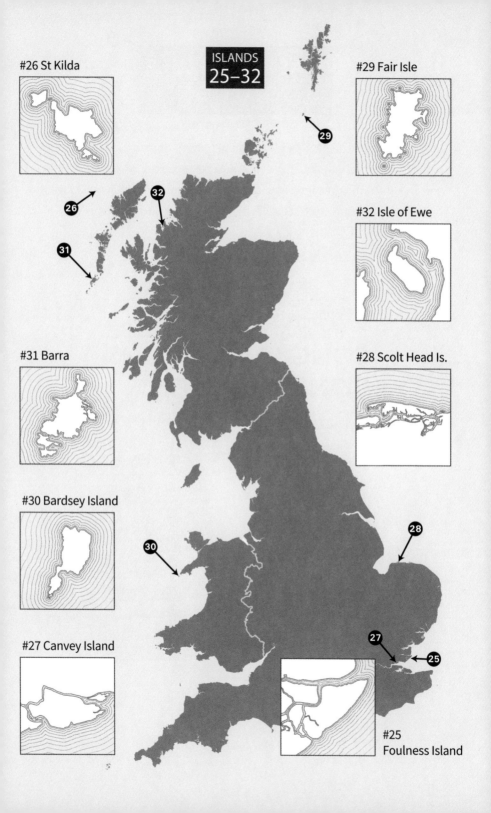

ISLANDS
25–32

#26 St Kilda

#29 Fair Isle

#32 Isle of Ewe

#31 Barra

#28 Scolt Head Is.

#30 Bardsey Island

#27 Canvey Island

#25
Foulness Island

MASTER PUZZLE SOLUTION

Read the numbers in each box from top to bottom as follows: the first number indicates the map number, the second number indicates the question number, and the third number indicates a letter index into that solution. Take the indicated letters from each solution, therefore taking one letter from each map, to spell out:

CONGRATULATIONS ON COMPLETING TOUR OF BRITAIN

ORDNANCE SURVEY MAPS INFORMATION

Each section of this book features five maps in the same order: a historical map; a town plan; an OS Explorer map; an OS Landranger map; and an OS Road map.

The historical maps were all originally published by Ordnance Survey between 1895 and 1908, and have been hand coloured by our cartographers.

The town plans use OS OpenMap Local, an open data product which is free to view, download and use for commercial, education and personal purposes. Please see the OS website for more details.

The remaining three map styles will be more familiar to the regular OS leisure map user:

OS Explorer

1: 25 000 (4 cm to 1 km or 2½ inches to the mile)

OS Explorer is Great Britain's most popular leisure map. It features footpaths, rights of way and open access land, and is recommended for walking, running and horse riding. It covers a smaller area than the OS Landranger map, but presents the landscape in more detail, aiding navigation and making it the perfect accompaniment on an adventure. It also highlights tourist information and points of interest, including viewpoints and pubs.

OS Landranger

1: 50 000 (2 cm to 1 km or 1¼ inches to the mile)

OS Landranger aids the planning of the perfect short break in Great Britain, and is a vital resource for identifying attractions and opportunities in both towns and countryside. It displays larger areas of the country than the OS Explorer, map, but in less detail, making it more suitable for touring by car or by bicycle, helping you access the best an area has to offer.

OS Road

1:250 000 (1 cm to 2.5 km or 1 inch to 4 miles)

The OS Road series helps you get to your destination. The range covers the whole of Great Britain and shows all motorways, primary routes and A roads plus detailed tourist information including National Parks, World Heritage Sites and a useful town and city gazetteer.

OS SHEET INDEX

Puzzle map		OS map sheet			Feature	1 km reference		
1	Isles of Scilly	101	203	7	Sir Cloudesley Shovell's grave	SV	92	10
2	Swanage, Isle of Purbeck	OL15	195	8	Town Hall	SZ	02	78
3	Athelney, Somerset	140	193	7	King Alfred's Monument	ST	34	29
4	Dartmoor	OL28	191	7	Grimspound	SX	70	80
5	Cotswold Hills	179	163	7	Cooper's Hill, Brockworth	SO	89	14
6	Blaenau Ffestiniog	OL18	115	6	Llechwedd Slate Mines	SH	69	46
7	Carmarthen	177	159	6	Carmarthen Castle	SN	41	19
8	Rhayader, Mid Wales	200	147	6	River Wye	SN	96	67
9	Gower, South Wales	164	159	6	Paviland Cave	SS	43	85
10	Menai Strait, North Wales	OL17	114	6	Menai Bridge	SH	55	71
11	Edge Hill, Liverpool	275	108	4	Railway station	SJ	37	89
12	Carlisle	315	85	4	Market Cross	NY	40	56
13	Norden, near Rochdale	OL21	109	4	Greenbooth Reservoir	SD	85	15
14	Silverdale	OL7	97	4	Warton Crag	SD	49	72
15	Eastern Lake District	OL5	90	4	High Street Roman Road	NY	44	10
16	Fort Augustus	416	34	2	Caledonian Canal	NH	37	09
17	Edinburgh	350	66	3	Old Town	NT	25	73
18	Oban	359	49	3	McCaig's Tower	NM	86	30
19	Unst, Shetland Islands	470	1	1	Keen of Hamar	HP	64	09
20	Black Isle	432	27	1	Chanonry Point	NH	74	56
21	York	290	105	4	Layerthorpe	SE	61	52
22	Wakefield	289	104	4	Wakefield	SE	33	20
23	Hawes	OL30	98	4	Hardraw Force	SD	86	91
24	Wooler	OL16	75	3	Peel Tower	NU	00	26
25	Cleveland Hills	OL26	93	4	Roseberry Topping	NZ	57	12
26	Bournville	220	139	5	Bournville factory	SP	04	81
27	Nottingham	260	129	5	Nottingham trams	SK	57	39
28	Youlgreave (Youlgrave)	OL24	119	4	Well Dressing, Main Street	SK	20	64
29	Scampton	272	121	4	Scampton Airfield	SK	96	79
30	Wenlock Edge	217	127	6	Ironbridge Gorge	SJ	67	03
31	King's Lynn	236	132	5	Alexandra Dock	TF	61	20
32	Colchester	184	168	5	Roman Town	TL	99	25
33	Coltishall	OL40	134	5	Limit of Navigation	TG	26	19
34	Minsmere	212	156	5	Nature Reserve	TM	47	67
35	The Brecks	229	144	5	Grime's Graves	TL	81	89
36	Seven Dials, London	173	176	8	Sundial monument	TQ	30	81
37	Oxford	180	164	8	Radcliffe Square	SP	51	06
38	Trosley Country Park	148	188	8	Pilgrim's Way	TQ	63	61
39	River Adur, West Sussex	OL11	198	8	Bramber Castle	TQ	18	10
40	Isle of Sheppey, Kent	149	178	8	Sheerness	TQ	91	75

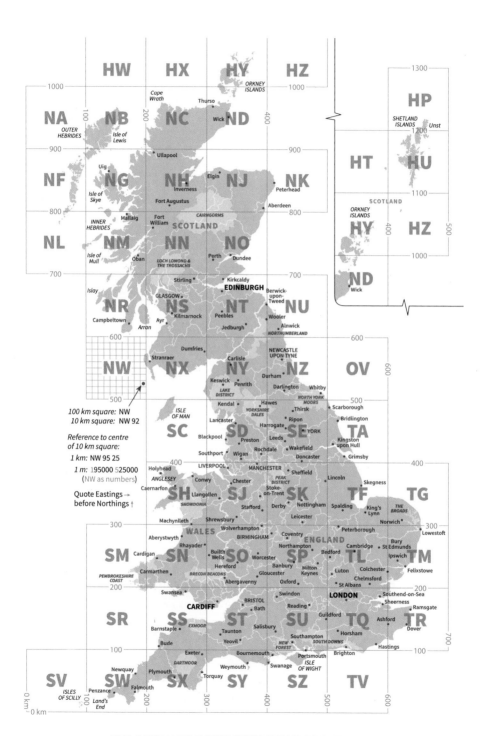

THE ORDNANCE SURVEY PUZZLE TOUR OF BRITAIN

CREDITS

Trapeze would like to thank everyone at Orion who worked on the publication of *The Ordnance Survey Puzzle Tour of Britain* in the UK.

Editorial: Anna Valentine, Grace Paul, Ru Merritt. **Copy editor:** Lindsay Davies. **Proof reader:** Patrick McConnell. **Contracts:** Anne Goddard, Paul Bulos. **Design:** Rabab Adams, Helen Ewing, Clare Sivell, Joanna Ridley, Nick May, Julyan Bayes. **Finance:** Jennifer Muchan, Jasdip Nandra, Afeera Ahmed, Elizabeth Beaumont, Sue Baker. **Marketing:** Katie Moss, Tom Noble. **Production:** Claire Keep, Fiona McIntosh. **Publicity:** Alainna Hadjigeorgiou. **Sales:** Jen Wilson, Esther Waters, Rachael Hum, Ellie Kyrke-Smith, Viki Cheung, Dominic Smith, Barbara Ronan, Maggy Park. **Rights:** Susan Howe, Richard King, Krystyna Kujawinska, Jessica Purdue. **Operations:** Jo Jacobs, Sharon Willis, Lisa Pryde.

ACKNOWLEDGEMENTS

Thank you to the many people who have worked
hard to make this book happen, including:

Nick Giles, Lee Newton, Liz Beverley, Carolyne Lawton, Jim Goldsmith,
Angus Young, Keegan Wilson, Joss Harris, Jo Lines, Gemma Jones,
The OS Consumer Team, The OS Cartographic Production Team, Sean Conway,
The OS GetOutside Champions and The National Library of Scotland and CLS
Data Limited, Trapeze, Orion Publishing, Dr Gareth Moore and his assistants
Laura Jane Ayres, Elizabeth Crowdy, James Cummings and Philip Marlow.

Special thanks go to Mark Wolstenholme: this book would not
have been possible without this creative vision, his eye for
detail and his ongoing desire to ensure that every map looked
great, told a story, and could pose plenty of questions.

Provisions of maps 1, 6, 11, 21, 26, and 31 are courtesy of CLS
Data Limited - thanks to Chris Walker and Adam Harmer.

Provision of OS Historical maps 16 and 36 are courtesy of the
National Library of Scotland – thanks to Craig Statham.

Ordnance Survey

Fancy brushing up on your map reading skills and solving an array of fiendish puzzles? Why not get yourself a copy of *The Ordnance Survey Puzzle Book* and pit your wits against Britain's greatest map makers?

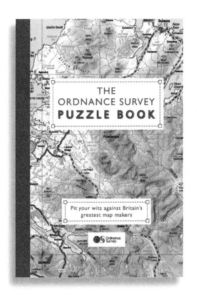

Share your adventures and puzzle-solving with us:

os.uk/blog

@ordnancesurvey

@OSLeisure

@osmapping

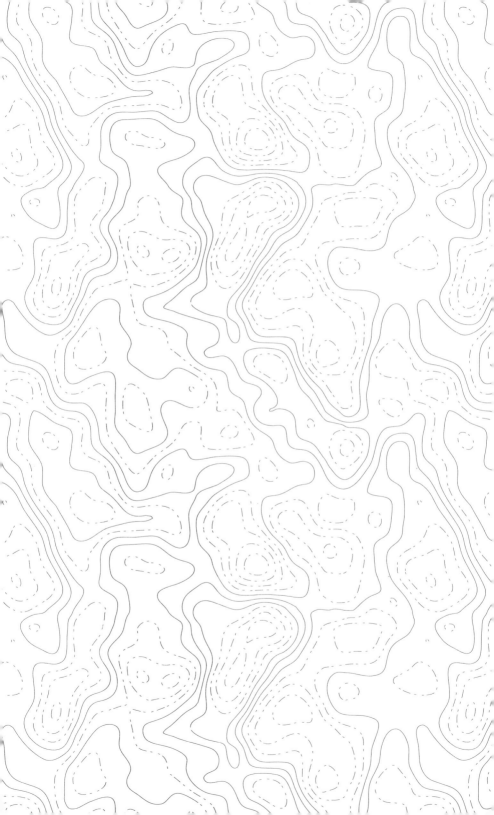